Lesbos

AEGEAN SEA

Chios

Smyrna

Samos

ndros

Ikaria

Dodecanese

Delos

Patmos

Paros

des

Naxos

Calymnos

Cos

Bay of Cos

ohnos

Antiparos

Ios

Nissyros

elos

RHODES

Santorin

Anaphi

Christianon

Karpathos

SEA OF CRETE

Amnisos

Heraklion

Pseira

Palaikastro

Tylissos

Mallia

Kato Zakro

Mt Ida

Mt Juktas

Knossos

Mt Dikte

CRETE

Phaistos

Koumasa

Printed in the Netherlands
by Drukkerij de Lange/van Leer N.V. Deventer

ATLANTIS

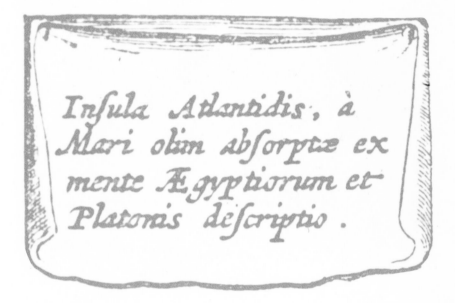

Insula Atlantidis, à Mari olim absorptæ ex mente Ægyptiorum et Platonis descriptio.

Insula Atlantis.

ATLANTIS

The truth behind the legend

A. G. GALANOPOULOS
and EDWARD BACON

NELSON

THOMAS NELSON AND SONS LTD
36 Park Street London W1
P.O. Box 336 Apapa Lagos
P.O. Box 25012 Nairobi
77 Coffee Street San Fernando Trinidad

Thomas Nelson (Australia) Ltd
597 Little Collins Street Melbourne C1

Thomas Nelson and Sons (South Africa) Proprietary Ltd
P.O. Box 9881 Johannesburg

Thomas Nelson and Sons (Canada) Ltd
81 Curlew Drive Don Mills Ontario

Thomas Nelson and Sons
Copewood and Davis Streets Camden 3, N.J.

Contents

Colour Plates

INTRODUCTION

INTRODUCTION
The Source
of the Legend

This book has been planned and written as a solution to the puzzle of Atlantis—what it was, where and when it was, and how it came to an end and was lost in the mists of the past. Since what is essentially new here derives from the work of a seismologist, concerned mainly with earthquake and volcanic processes, our approach and solution to the problem are geophysical. Others, notably Professor Spyridon Marinatos, have approached the same problem from historical and archaeological angles and have reached very similar conclusions. Professor Marinatos is almost certainly the most distinguished Greek archaeologist living and is at present the head of the Greek archaeological services. His excavations have been mainly concerned with Minoan and Mycenaean sites. Perhaps the most sensational in recent years were those which uncovered two untouched beehive tombs not far from Pylos and revealed, among other treasures, two splendid inlaid daggers and great quantities of the finest gem-seals; and over the years he has been seeking a physical explanation for the catastrophic break-up of the Minoan civilization. In the spring of 1967 he put his theories to the test in an excavation near Akrotiri on Thera —with immediate success, as will appear later in this book.

Science is indivisible; and it is a source of immense satisfaction when the archaeologist and the geophysicist can go forward hand in hand. But since the climax of the story of Atlantis and the reasons for its being a problem at all are geophysical ones, it seems that the central solution must be based on geophysical fact, scientifically discovered and scientifically proved.

There can be few subjects with so extensive a bibliography as Atlantis and the problem of its submergence. In the centuries since Plato, scientists in practically every field, poets, political philosophers, idealists, devoted amateurs, writers of all kinds, even metaphysicians, have concerned themselves with the tragic story. There are many and good reasons why this should be so; it is a puzzling, fascinating and moving story. But the sway which it has had over so many different kinds of men and the strange courses to which it has driven them seem to suggest that it answers some deep-seated human need. It appeals perhaps to a kind of nostalgic poetry which lies deep in nearly every human being, it is the lost paradise, the Garden of Eden, the Golden Age, the cradle of mankind, the remote and intangible theatre in which all the wish-fulfilment roles can be played out without inhibition, the great 'if only . . .' country. And yet behind it lies a perfectly respectable ancestry. It makes its first appearance in the austere and intellectual pages of Plato, the perfect 'Establishment' author, and it is a subject with which the highest intellects can relax without shame. And since, at first sight, it seems so cut off from the dullness and restrictions of reality, it is the perfect field for those relaxed intellects to suffuse and expand with dreams and fantasies and so to identify it, most passionately, with their secret wishes and ideals. Atlantis has fragmented into innumerable concepts, subjectively engendered and passionately nurtured; developing moreover a vast secondary literature of confutation, defence and the pursuit of the innumerable hares of controversy. The wood has become lost in the trees.

What is the wood—that is, the basic story? It occurs in one author only —and nowhere else. It is found in two of Plato's dialogues, the *Timaeus* and the *Critias*. These were planned as a trilogy and supposedly took place during the three days following the dialogue which we call the *Republic*. They were also planned as developments of themes arising out of that dialogue. The *Timaeus* is complete and is one of Plato's greatest works, concerned with the creation of the universe. The second dialogue, the *Critias*, is incomplete, breaking off suddenly in the passage which concerns Atlantis. The third dialogue, which would have been called *Hermocrates*, was apparently never written.

Since the sole sources of the story are the passages in the *Timaeus* and the *Critias* and, in consequence, any explanation of the story must be based upon them, and since we believe that many readers must be more familiar with the speculations on this evidence than with the evidence itself, we reprint in full the relevant passages of the two dialogues in Appendix A. Frequent quotations from these dialogues will appear throughout the book as necessary; but Plato's whole story is a fascinating one, and it is right that the reader should have the whole of it conveniently available. This book is, very largely, a story of detection; the solution is only valid if it satisfies the whole of the evidence.

Plato tells the whole story—with its inherent problems. In the chapters that follow we shall show what we believe to be the irrefutable solution.

In 1926 the Frenchmen J. Gattefossé and C. Roux published a bibliography on Atlantis with an estimated total of 1,700 works. Since then the number has risen considerably and may well have reached 5,000. The writers of these works fall into four main categories:

(1) Those who accept Plato's story as perfectly true.

(2) Those who believe that Atlantis did exist, but not in the Atlantic Ocean, and who suggest various other localities.

(3) Those who claim that the Atlantis story is a compilation of legends and historical facts relating to various peoples and different ages.

(4) Those who believe that the story is fictitious and an invention by Plato

Plato, whose account of Atlantis is the source of the legend. This Roman portrait bust is a copy of a Greek original that was probably made by a contemporary of Plato.

to give a framework to certain politico-philosophical ideas, as More did in *Utopia* and Butler in *Erewhon*.

Aristotle was the first of those of the fourth class, and this is hardly surprising. He was the first great pragmatic scientist. He could no doubt perceive in the story all its geophysical problems, without at that time having the means to solve them.

The writers in the second and third classes will be dealt with in due course. It is necessary now to state and establish the belief that Plato was telling what he believed to be historical truth.

In the first place, he says so flatly, no less than four times. Critias says at the start:

'Listen then, Socrates, to a tale which, though passing strange, is yet wholly true, as Solon, the wisest of the Seven, once upon a time declared.'

After Critias' introduction of the story, Socrates says:

'Excellent. But come now, what was this exploit described by Critias, following Solon's report, as a thing not verbally reported, although actually performed by this city long ago?'

Later, when describing how he first heard the story, Critias says:

'"Tell us from the beginning," said Amynander, "what Solon related and how, and who were the informants who vouched for its truth."'

And at the end of Critias' narration, Socrates says:

'And the fact that it is not invented fable but a genuine history is all important.'

Thus Plato makes four direct statements that the story is true historical fact. However, those who believe that the story is a myth claim that in this Plato was disingenuous and had two objects in view. First, he wished (so they maintain) to excuse Critias for his despotism as one of the Thirty Tyrants, showing him as influenced by his grandfather, Critias the Elder, who ascribed the power and prosperity of Athens to the monarchical system which existed there at the time of Atlantis; and, secondly, that Plato wished to clear Socrates of the charge that it was he who inspired his pupil Critias with despotic ideas.

This seems far-fetched. Quite apart from the fact that it would be an extremely ineffective way of achieving either object there would be little point in stressing over and over again that the story was fact and not fiction, since the veracity or otherwise of the story of the submersion of Atlantis could have little bearing on Plato's political and philosophical ideas.

Again, even supposing that Plato did require an imaginary country outside the then-known world, it was hardly necessary for him to give a detailed description of the way the metropolis of that country was fortified. Further, the description of those fortifications and of the political life of the inhabitants of Atlantis does not paint a picture of an ideal state, nor

14

for that matter of a consistent one, from the philosophical point of view. If Plato had required Atlantis as an example of an ideal polity he would hardly have extolled the Athenians for the war of liberation which they waged against Atlantis (see *Timaeus*, *23C*).

Again, according to Proclus (AD 410–85), Crantor, a commentator on Plato who lived three centuries after him, had been shown panels bearing hieroglyphic inscriptions recording the story of Atlantis by the priests of the goddess Neith, who had founded Sais.

Yet again, a man inventing a convenient myth makes it logical and self-consistent. But Plato himself is worried by certain aspects of the story. Critias says (*Crit.*, *118C*): 'Now as regards the depth of this trench and its breadth and length, it seems incredible that it should be so large as the account states, considering that it was made by the hand, and in addition to all the other operations, but none the less we must report what we heard.' In any case what has incredible civil engineering to do with politico-philosophical myth? These are obviously not the accents of a fabulist but the puzzled questionings of someone concerned with something reported as historical fact.

It is sometimes objected that Plato spent thirteen years in Egypt and would surely have been able to have collected more precise information about Atlantis from the Egyptian priests. Had he been Herodotus no doubt he would have attempted this; but he was a philosopher, not an historian. Further, it is generally believed that his visit to Egypt took place a number of years before the writing of the *Timaeus*. The Atlantis story, though so interesting to us, was not necessarily so to him, and is in fact only a short and minor part of the *Timaeus* dialogue.

And finally there is the point that the Atlantis story was not preserved purely by word of mouth, as might be supposed. In the *Critias*, Critias says: 'And these writings [of Solon] were in the possession of my grandfather and are actually now in mine.'

It is therefore quite clear that the story of Atlantis in the original form that we know is not an invention of Plato but an actual story brought from Egypt by Solon; and Plato, realizing that it might be considered as a myth, wished to forestall such an eventuality and, in the *Timaeus* alone, flatly states four times that the story is indeed true.

To what then does this story amount? Is it credible? Is it consistent? And if not, what are its incredibilities and what its inconsistencies?

WHAT PLATO MEANT AND SAID

ONE
The Cultural Aspects of Plato's Atlantis

Leaving the geographical nature, size and location of Atlantis until the next chapter let us now consider what sort of a civilization it is that Plato describes.

In the first place its destruction took place at a time when it was contemplating a war of aggression against Athens and Egypt simultaneously; and also an Athenian army was destroyed by a natural calamity during the operations. Therefore Atlantis was an organized militaristic state, capable of mounting large-scale seaborne operations and contemporary with an Athens and an Egypt which were similarly competent and organized.

Secondly, Atlantis had a highly organized agriculture. To quote the *Critias*:

'It produced and brought to perfection all those sweet-scented stuffs which the earth produces now, whether made of roots or herbs or trees, or of liquid gums derived from flowers or fruits. The cultivated fruit also [vines], and the dry [corn], which serves us for nutriment and all the other kinds that we use for our meals—the various species of which are comprehended under the name "vegetables"—and all the produce of trees which affords liquid and solid food and unguents, and the fruit of the orchard trees, so hard to store, which is grown for the sake of amusement and pleasure, and all the after-dinner fruits which we serve up as welcome remedies for the sufferer from repletion—all these that hallowed island as it lay then beneath the sun produced in marvellous beauty and endless abundance' (*Crit., 115A–B*).

And that this was not an accident of paradise is made clear a little later: 'And they cropped the land twice a year, making use of rains from Heaven in the winter, and the waters that issue from the earth in summer, by conducting the streams from the trenches.' Therefore Atlantis had a rich and varied agricultural produce, regularly cropped and systematically irrigated.

Thirdly, Atlantis was a place of conscious amenity, leisure and public services. Again, in the *Critias*:

'The springs they made use of, one kind being of cold, another of warm water, were of abundant volume, and each kind was wonderfully well adapted for use because of the natural taste and excellence of its waters;

and these they surrounded with buildings and with plantations of trees such as suited the waters; and, moreover, they set reservoirs round about, some under the open sky, and others under cover to supply hot baths in the winter; they put separate baths for the King and for the private citizens, besides others for women, and others again for horses and all other beasts of burden, fitting out each in appropriate manner. And the outflowing water they conducted to the sacred grove of Poseidon, which contained trees of all kinds that were of marvellous beauty and height because of the richness of the soil; and by means of channels they led the waters to the outer circles over against the bridges. And there they had constructed many temples for gods, and many gardens and many exercising grounds.'

The implications of this passage are many and extraordinary. In social organization it indicates a monarchical and class system, and a specialized status for women. It indicates likewise practice and skill in hydraulic engineering and bridge-building; a knowledge of the pleasure and use of bathing which is extended even to animals; the use of horses as domestic animals; the planting of trees and making of gardens; the construction of reservoirs and buildings associated with them; and a complex theogony, since temples are built for *many* gods. Perhaps most important of all, this is shown to be a *leisured* society, for the gardens and exercising grounds are the amenities of a leisured and not a subsistence community. The man who is struggling for existence has neither the need nor the wish for 'exercise'; and even today it is only the rich farmer who bothers much about gardens.

Fourthly, Plato's Atlantis was a literate state. The mutual relations of the ten kings 'were governed by the precepts of Poseidon, as handed down to them by the law and by the records *inscribed* by the first prince on a pillar of orichalcum, which was placed within the temple of Poseidon in the centre of the island'.

This leads, through its mention of orichalcum (an alloy of copper), to the fifth aspect of Atlantis—that it was a metal-working civilization. Two passages in the *Critias* show this:

'And they covered with brass, as though with a plaster, all the circumference of the wall which surrounded the outermost circle; and that of the inner one they covered with tin; and that which encompassed the acropolis itself with orichalcum which sparkled like fire' (*116 B–C*).

And a little later:

'All the exterior of the temple they coated with silver save only the pinnacles, and these they coated with gold. As to the exterior, they made the roof all of ivory in appearance, variegated with gold and silver and orichalcum and all the rest of the walls and pillars and floors they covered with orichalcum.'

Therefore the inhabitants knew of the use of copper and tin, and bronze, the alloy of these two metals. They also knew and used gold and silver.

Finally there are one or two significant points in relation to architecture. The metropolis of Atlantis is described as being enclosed by a circle of huge walls 50 stadia in radius, or about 10,000 yards. This sounds like the mega-lithic monuments which have appeared in various parts of the ancient world at differing dates. And it is also worth recording at this point that 'the stone they quarried beneath the central island all round, and from beneath the outer and inner circles, some of it being white, some black and some red . . . and of the buildings some they framed in one simple colour, in others they wove a pattern of many colours by blending the stones for the sake of ornament . . .'.

Now, to anyone even superficially acquainted with the great Bronze Age civilizations which the archaeologists have revealed to us—such as those of Egypt, Mesopotamia, the Indus Valley, the Hittites, the Minoans and the Mycenaeans—Plato's Atlantis must immediately appear as a Bronze Age civilization. In other words, one of those splendid periods of history to which all legends hark back as the Golden Age, when luxury, fertility, prosperity and international exchange of goods and ideas seemed to promise a glowing and unending prospect of happiness. These great periods all fell within the great Second Millennium—the years between 2000 and 1000 BC—although some of them started earlier and some continued a little longer; and their scope and nature are admirably summarized in Geoffrey Bibby's *Four Thousand Years Ago*.

They are lands of surplus—communities in which for one reason or another man can easily produce more than he needs, where he has in consequence acquired leisure to think, to enjoy himself, to express himself in religion, art and the *douceur de vivre*. In Egypt, Mesopotamia and the Indus Valley, it is the equable climate and the seemingly endless benison of fertility annually renewed by fresh silt brought down by the great rivers. Elsewhere it is in the possession of desirable or useful metals and minerals —copper, tin, gold, silver, lapis lazuli—or the ability to sail ships and to trade in such desirable substances.

It is the first great age of organization and specialization. As man has moved into towns and cities, it has become obviously sensible to apportion tasks to those who can do them well: the agriculturalist grows crops, the herdsman breeds and tends cattle, the metalworker and the potter ply their crafts not only for themselves but for the whole public; the community builds and operates the drains of a city, controls and distributes the flood waters of the fertilizing rivers, builds and administers public places of use and amenity, like markets, gardens, bathing places, and, by an inevitable process, trains and employs those who are necessary to administer, control and protect all such services—creates, in other words, a civil service, a police and an army.

But who is 'the community' in this creative aspect? Usually what may be termed the priest-king—the representative of the godhead, the divine accident, so to speak, which has created the prime moving fertility of the civilization—the sun, the fertilizing waters, the principles of reproduction

The Great Bath of Mohenjodaro in the Indus valley, a Bronze Age building that echoes Plato's account of the baths of Atlantis.

which ensure the continuity of human, animal and vegetable life, even the principle of strength needed to control all such things, whether embodied in the bull or the lion, or such subtle beasts as the snake, or such compound animals as the sphinx and the griffin. As life becomes more complex or more precarious, this representative 'priest–king' of the community may change. He may become more priestly or in times of danger more like a warrior. He may subdivide himself into an oligarchy or a bureaucracy or the equivalent of a feudal system; or just as life has become more complex for the ordinary man, so too it may for the god, whose different aspects become different gods, and out of a single deity grows out a whole pantheon of gods.

But gods and kings alike demand respect and deserve honour. Out of the surplus of the great Bronze Age civilizations, respect and honour are heaped upon the gods and kings in forms which are material as well as spiritual. Temples and palaces are built; statues are carved; rich textiles, elaborate jewellery, splendid furniture, ritual vessels are created in ever-increasing quantity, richness and beauty.

Ceremonials, rituals and sports come into being, music and dancing—and indeed all of these are the outcome of the individual's desire to do honour to the 'priest–king'; 'We must love the highest when we see it' and, like the *Jongleur de Notre Dame*, choose our own special skill to display that love.

Yet the highest, the 'priest–king', is mortal: but the principle of the priest–king cannot be allowed to be other than immortal; and from this, it seems, springs the whole concept of immortality. The king must die; but the king cannot die; the king does not die, but lives for ever, not only

The semi-divine majesty of the priest-king, representative of the godhead and symbol of the community: gigantic statue of Rameses II from Abu Simbel.

The sumptuous grave-goods of the royal burials of the Bronze Age: the skull of a court lady of Ur surrounded by gold and other valuables (*left*); jewellery from a grave in the Royal Cemetery at Ur (*below left*).

in his successor but also in himself, in a life after death. And not only does the king live on, so do all his subjects. Great tombs are built for kings and nobles, stocked with the 'grave-goods', the necessities of life hereafter— weapons, clothes, food and drink, rich jewels, beds and thrones, cosmetics, pets and domestic animals, servants and concubines (sometimes sacrificed to accompany their master, but more often shown as models or pictorial representations). The sheer money value of these ostentatious and costly funerals can be seen in the treasures of Tutankhamûn's tomb. But the principle is the same in the simpler burials—the child with his single

Bronze Age warfare, organized on a large scale, still depended heavily upon the semi-divine leadership of King or Pharaoh: in this temple carving from Abu Simbel, Rameses II is shown slaying the enemies of Egypt.

toy, the adult with a couple of cooking pots, a dagger, a brooch or a couple of jars of eye- or lip-paint.

From the ruins of buildings the organization of these towns can be deduced, from the requirements of the soul in the life after death the habits of daily life can be recreated. And the generalized picture of the Bronze Age which emerges is one which is so close in general outlines to Plato's Atlantis that it is difficult to disagree with the statement of Professor Gidon of Caen that 'the Atlantis civilization described by Plato is indeed a civilization of the Bronze Age'.

To follow on the outline of aspects of Plato's Atlantis summarized on pp. 19-21, let us, in the same order, seek them in the great Bronze Age civilizations.

Although some of these—notably, for long periods, Crete and the Indus Valley—seem to have enjoyed almost total freedom from war and the

Flourishing agriculture, described by Plato in his account of Atlantis, was a feature of most Bronze Age cultures: men with flails, depicted on the 'Harvester Vase' from Knossos (*left*); the giant *pithoi* and storage pits of the palace of Knossos (*below left*); and the enormous brick granaries of Mohenjodaro (*right*).

necessities of defence, others such as the Egyptians, the Hittites and the earlier Assyrians were organized as states with armies both offensive and defensive. Military operations are frequent in the Middle East; and the innumerable inscriptions of the victories of Rameses II in the fourteenth century BC, however unreliable in detail, do at least attest a world of organized military operations on a very large scale. Sea-borne trade was already well established—copper and tin were sought wherever they could be found, in Cyprus, in Spain and in Britain, and carried by sea; there was extensive trade between Mesopotamia and the Indus Valley and (perhaps) Oman through the *entrepôt* of Bahrein. And that these ships could be used for naval invasion became apparent towards the end of the era when Rameses III had to repel an invasion of the Sea Peoples in the first great sea-battle recorded in history.

For agriculture, we need hardly say more than that great civilizations cannot exist without it; and the complex cultivation of the Indus, Nile and Euphrates–Tigris valleys in the Bronze Age provided all the classic information on arable farming of the Second Millennium that man could desire.

Successful agriculture leads inevitably to prosperity, leisure and the need for organization and public services; and the corn bin of the Neo-lithic farmer grows by inevitable progression to the vast public granaries of Harappa and Mohenjodaro or the storehouses of Minoan Knossos, with their huge and splendid *pithoi* of grain and oil and wine. And out of organization and control spring power and the delegation of power, the growth of a system of rule, the king or the high-priest and his deputies,

civil or religious. In Crete Minos succeeds Minos, in Egypt Pharaoh follows Pharaoh, and the Hittite kings reverberate in liquid polysyllables. In Sumer the early religion-based communism breaks up under the spread of private property and dynasties of kings and powerful magistrates emerge from anonymity.

The first architect, Imhotep, the builder of the Step Pyramid, had died about a thousand years before the beginning of the era we are studying and had indeed already become a legend and a god. Who was the first hydraulic engineer is as obscure as what song the sirens sang: but his genius, like that of the man who invented the wheel, is apparent throughout the great riverine Bronze Age kingdoms—in the elaborate drains of Harappa and Mohenjodaro, in the docks of Lothal, in the levees and irrigation canals of Mesopotamia and the water management and nilometers of Egypt.

Pets (mostly dogs and monkeys) and domestic animals (mainly cattle, sheep and goats) are common throughout the Bronze Age; and it is around the middle of the Second Millennium that the horse and the chariot appear in the Middle East with the arrival of Indo-European-speaking peoples from South Russia and from the East. With the Aryans comes the horse, the property and symbol of nobility, for whom no treatment is too good, no adornment too luxurious.

For the planting of trees and gardens, it is not easy to be precise; gardens and plantation leave few traces behind. The carbonized seeds of grapes, figs, olives, almonds and apples are found at many sites of remote antiquity; and although the probability is that many of them were cultivated, the evidence that they were so planted is difficult to find—while to be certain that they were so planted for pleasure is virtually impossible. It is generally believed that grapevines were planted on the slopes of Sumerian ziggurats for the express honour of the deity concerned; and from this to the much later hanging gardens of Babylon seems a logical progression.

Horse and chariot appear in the Middle East around the middle or the second millennium BC: gold seal from Mycenae, sixteenth century BC (*left*). Before the introduction of the horse, other domestic animals served similar purposes: plaster impression of a seal from Crete depicting a carriage drawn by two goats.

Cisterns and reservoirs for water appear in all those Bronze Age civilizations, whose first need is water—the condition of life and fertility—and whose supply is not as regular as their need.

On the origin of gods, the whole field of speculation is open; but the usual progress of man's belief in, or creation of, a divine power seems to begin with a simple god (or goddess) to match his first simple needs; to a proliferation of deities as his own needs become more complex; to a single divinity as the first stirrings of philosophy reach out to a single, overmastering principle of the universe. That the Bronze Age was a time of complexity is clear; and that it was a time of many gods is probable throughout and certain wherever literacy has appeared and belief is recorded—especially in Mesopotamia and Egypt.

For the Bronze Age sees the birth and spread of literacy. Sumer and Mesopotamia generally provide a wealth of written material which can be read and understood. The Hittite scripts are yielding their secrets. Crete in this era had two scripts, the first, Linear A (as yet impenetrable), and the second, Linear B, now revealed by Ventris and Chadwick to be syllabic writing of a primitive Greek. Other races of this era, in India and the Eastern Mediterranean, likewise wrote records, business transactions and signatures—which may be terse but are nevertheless the symbols of the mechanical memory which is the first product of literacy.

The Bronze Age was not only a metal-working age but was also the first age in which metal was used on a considerable scale. Certain metals, notably gold and copper, occur in a free state and can be beaten into shapes with little difficulty; and the centuries before the Bronze Age are known as the Chalcolithic or Aenolithic Age—the copper-cum-stone age. But it is in the Bronze Age that the combination of copper and tin into

The Bronze Age saw the birth of literacy, with a variety of scripts and other forms of writing being developed in Egypt, Mesopotamia, and other centres of civilization. Among them were the scripts of Crete, Linear A (*left*) and Linear B.

the hard and useful alloy known as bronze becomes general and the trade in metals and tools develops a way of life. Gold and silver are widely used —in sheet, in filigree, in granulation, alone or in combination, incrusted with precious and semi-precious stones, inlaid with black niello or blue lapis lazuli or frit or red carnelian. And these metals are used with a prodigality that seems incredible—the treasures of the Royal Tombs of Ur and the splendours of Tutankhamûn's magnificent obsequies are evidence enough. And these are the lucky survivors that escaped the robbers and the re-melt. For these metals, unlike pottery and stone, can be melted down and used over and over again in unrecognizable transformations. Who is to say that your wedding ring does not contain a grain or two of the gold of Sumer? What was the *total* of any Bronze Age treasury at any given moment is impossible to say and teasing to imagine.

We have plenty of evidence of their buildings: the vast brick platforms of Harappa and Mohenjodaro, in Mesopotamia even, where there is no stone, the vast mounds that survive of mud-brick temples and ziggurats, in Egypt the great tombs and temples (the great pyramids are all earlier), in Crete and Greece the megalithic tombs and monuments, those constructions of great stones which were to be the signature of the progress of Aegean traders throughout the Western Mediterranean and far out on to the Atlantic coasts of Spain, France and Britain.

Indeed there is nothing in the essence of Plato's Atlantis that cannot be matched in the known remains of the high Bronze Age; and it is impossible to read his account without being sure that what is being described is indeed a Bronze Age civilization—perhaps one that we know not of, possibly one that we know under another name.

Some of the great buildings of the Bronze Age survive, though often ruinous; the ziggurat of Ur (*below*) originally towered several times as high as the brick mound that stands today in the Mesopotamian plain. The temple of Queen Hatshepsut (*right*) at Deir el-Bahri is among the most imposing buildings of the Bronze Age.

TWO
The Geography of Plato's Atlantis

This, then, was the kind of civilization that Plato described. What were its geographical and physical features, what was its period in history and what its origins and end?

These are all fairly clearly stated, once the initial problems of whether Atlantis was a single large island or a kingdom of two or more islands is resolved. Fortunately this becomes quite clear in the *Critias*. In the legendary distribution of the earth among the gods, Poseidon received an island on which dwelt one of the first of mortals, Evenor, with his wife Leucippe and their daughter Cleito. After the death of Evenor and Leucippe, Poseidon married Cleito;

'And he begat five pairs of twin sons and reared them up; and when he had divided all the island of Atlantis into ten portions, he assigned to the first born of the eldest sons his mother's dwelling and the allotment surrounding it which was the largest and best; and him he appointed to be king over the rest, and the others to be rulers, granting to each the rule over many men and a large tract of country and to all of them he gave names, giving to him that was eldest and king the name after which the whole island was called and the sea spoken of as the Atlantic, because the first king who then reigned had the name of Atlas' (*Crit.*, *113E–114A*).

At several points in the *Critias*, Plato gives a detailed description of the metropolis, the dwelling place, that is, of the mother of Atlas, eldest son of Poseidon and first king of Atlantis:

'Bordering on the sea and extending through the centre of the whole island there was a plain, which is said to have been the fairest of all plains and highly fertile; and moreover, near the plain, over against its centre, at a distance of about 50 stades[1] [i.e. 10,000 yards] there stood a mountain that was low on all sides . . . (and to make the hill whereon Leucippe dwelt impregnable, Poseidon) . . . broke it off all round about; and he made circular belts of sea and land enclosing one another alternately, some greater, some smaller, two being of land and three of sea, which he carved as it were out of the midst of the island; and these belts were at even distances on all sides, so as to be impassable for man' (*Crit.*, *113C–D*).

Poseidon, legendary founder of Atlantis: head of a bronze statue now in Athens, *c*. 460 BC.

[1] The Greek stade was 600 Greek feet, i.e. just over 200 yards.

These 'circular belts of sea' must be regarded as concentric canals of waters, and there were three of them. How this was achieved is described in three later passages:

'First of all they bridged over the circles of sea which surrounded the Ancient Metropolis, making thereby a road towards and from the royal palace. And they had built the palace at the very beginning where the settlement was first made by their god and their ancestors; and each King received it from his predecessor . . .

'For beginning at the sea, they bored a channel right through to the outermost circle which was three plethra [100 yards] in breadth, one hundred feet in depth, and 50 stades [10,000 yards] in length and thus they made the entrance to it from the sea like that to a harbour by opening out a mouth large enough for the greater ships to sail through' (*Crit.*, *115D*).

'The greatest of the circles with which a boring was made for the sea was three stades [600 yards] in breadth and the circle of land next to it was of equal breadth; and of the second pair of circles that of water was two stades [400 yards] in breadth and that of dry land equal again to the preceding one of water; and the circle which ran round the central island

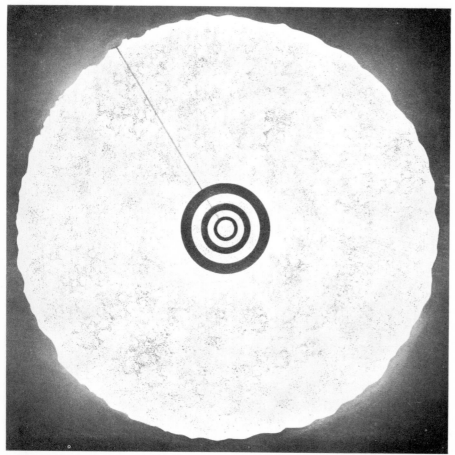

The Ancient Metropolis of Atlantis, as described in Plato's *Critias*.

itself was of one stade's breadth [200 yards]. And this island wherein stood the royal palace was of five stades [1,000 yards] in diameter' (*Crit.*, *115E*).

These passages quite clearly show that the Ancient Metropolis was a small round island with a radius of about six miles.

After describing this Ancient Metropolis Plato continued with a description of Atlantis which, as will be seen, is very different from a circular island of 12 miles diameter.

'Now as regards the city and environs of the ancient dwelling we have now wellnigh completed the description as it was originally given. We must endeavour next to repeat *the account of the rest of the country*, what its natural character was, and in what fashion it was ordered. In the first place, then, according to the account, the whole region was sheer out of the sea to a great height, but the part about the city was all a smooth plain, enclosing it round about, and being itself encircled by mountains which stretched as far as the sea; and this plain had a level surface and was as a whole rectangular in shape, being 3000 stades [340 miles] long on either side and 2000 stades [227 miles] wide at its centre reckoning upwards from the sea. And this region all along the island faced towards the South and was sheltered from the Northern blasts. And the mountains which surrounded it were at that time celebrated as surpassing all that now exist in number, magnitude and beauty; for they had upon them rich villages of country folk, and streams and lakes and meadows which furnished ample nutriment to all the animals both tame and wild, and timber of various sizes and descriptions, abundantly sufficient for the needs of all and every craft. Now, as a result of natural forces, together with the labours of many kings which extended over many ages, the condition of the plain was this. It was originally a quadrangle, rectilinear for the most part and elongated; and what it lacked of this shape they made right by means of a trench dug round about it. Now, as regards the depth of this trench and its breadth and length, it seems incredible that it should be so large as the account states, considering that it was made by hand, and in addition to all the other operations, but none the less we must report what we heard; it was dug out to the depth of a plethrum [*c.* 97 ft] to a uniform breadth of a stade [200 yards], and since it was dug round the whole plain its consequent length was 10,000 stades [1,136 miles]. It received the streams which came down from the mountains and after circling round the plain and coming towards the city on this side and on that, it discharged them thereabouts into the sea. And on the island side of the city channels were cut in straight lines, of almost 100 ft in length, across the plain and these discharged themselves into the trench on the seaward side, the distance between each being 100 stades [12 miles]. It was in this way that they conveyed to the city the timber from the mountains and transported also on boats the season's products by cutting transverse passages from one channel to the next and also to the city. And they cropped the land twice a year, making use of the rain from Heaven in the winter; and the waters that issue from the earth in summer, by conducting the streams from the trenches' (*Crit., 118A–E*).

This passage is not crystal clear; and Plato obviously is not himself quite satisfied with it—as is apparent in his use of the phrase 'it seems incredible that it should be so large as the account states' and 'none the less we must report what we heard'. (Incidentally, these phrases are clear evidence, if such were still needed, that Plato considered the story somewhat indigestible fact and not easily digestible myth.) Nevertheless certain points are quite clear. The plain surrounding the city is approximately rectangular, the trench enclosing the plain being 10,000 stades (1,136 miles) in length and the greater side of the plain 3,000 stades (340 miles) long. Therefore the 2,000 stades (227 miles) mentioned by Plato refer to the breadth of the plain at its middle point and not to the distance from the centre of the plain to the sea, as some writers maintain.

Next, the plain surrounding the city does not appear to be the same as the one close to the Ancient Metropolis since this lay in the centre of the island at a distance of 50 stades (6 miles) from the sea. Whereas the plain surrounding the City was 3,000 stades (340 miles) long and 2,000 stades (227 miles) wide; and so the centre of this plain must have been very much more than six miles from the sea. The attempt to reconcile these statements by suggesting that the Ancient Metropolis was not in the centre of the island but close to the sea in the middle of one of the sides of the island likewise will not work in view of the passage (*Crit., 113D*) which states that the belts of water encircling the metropolis were everywhere equidistant from the centre of the island.

Finally, the plain round the City was enclosed by mountains whose slopes reached the sea. These mountains were famous, large and had many rich villages among them; and in consequence it is clear that the dimensions given by Plato (3,000 stades (340 miles) by 2,000 stades (227 miles)) refer only to the plain surrounding the City and not to the whole island, as some believe.

Continuing this description and with special bearing on the population of Atlantis, Plato says:

'As regards their manpower it was ordained that each allotment [*kleros*] should furnish one man as leader of all the men in the plain who were fit to bear arms and the size of the allotment was about ten times ten stades [10 × 2,000 yds, i.e. 20,000 sq. yds] and the total number of the allotments was sixty thousand; and the number of men in the mountains and in the rest of the country was countless, according to the report, and according to their districts and villages they were all assigned to these allotments under their leaders. So it was ordained that each such leader should provide for war the sixth part of a war-chariot's equipment, so as to make up 10,000 chariots in all, together with two horses and mounted men; also a pair of horses without a car, and attached thereto a com-

Greek *hoplites* (heavy armed infantrymen) such as Plato must have had in mind when using the term *hoplite* to describe the soldiers of Atlantis.

batant with a small shield and for charioteer the rider who springs from horse to horse; and two *hoplites* [heavy armed infantrymen]; and archers and slingers, two of each, and light-armed slingers and javelin men, three of each; and four sailors towards the manning of twelve hundred ships. Such then were the military dispositions of the Royal City; and those of the other nine varied in various ways, which it would take a long time to tell' (*Crit., 118E–119C*).

This passage establishes that the plain belonged to the 'Royal City' and that the inhabitants of the mountains and other parts of Atlantis were under different, but subordinate rulers. Atlantis, as already stated, had ten towns and ten rulers. The Royal City, as described by Plato in the above passages, was the capital of an area of 3,000 stades (340 miles) by 2,000 stades (227 miles). If the remaining nine cities referred to in the last sentence of the last-quoted passage were the capitals of similar areas, the dimensions of the whole state of Atlantis would have been in the neighbourhood of 30,000 stades (3,400 miles) by 20,000 stades (2,300 miles). These dimensions indicate a land mass of about the size of Asia Minor and inhabitable North Africa combined. The length of the Mediterranean is about 2,100 miles; and an island 3,400 miles long could not possibly be situated inside the Mediterranean basin.

Now Solon had travelled in the Mediterranean and was probably aware

37

of this difficulty. Round about this time the Phoenicians had circumnavigated Africa on the orders of the Pharaoh Necho (609–593 BC) and so were aware of the existence of the Atlantic. It is therefore possible that in his discussions with the priests of Sais, Solon may have pointed out that an island of the dimensions claimed for Atlantis could not be located in the Mediterranean; and that the priests, aware of the huge size of the recently discovered Atlantic Ocean, took the opportunity to place Atlantis in that ocean. And it may well be that it is from this that the Atlantic derives its name. It is worth noting that the Egyptian writings do not use the name 'Pillar of Hercules', and the priest of Sais is quoted as saying:

' "For the ocean there was at that time navigable; for in front of the mouth which you Greeks call, as you say, the pillars of Heracles, there lay an island which was larger than Libya and Asia together; and it was possible for the travellers of that time to cross from it to the other islands and from the islands to the whole of the continent over against them which encompasses that veritable ocean. For all that we have here, lying within the mouth of which we speak, what is evidently a haven having a narrow entrance; but that yonder is a real ocean, and the land surrounding it may most rightly be called, in the fullest and truest sense, a continent" ' (*Tim.*, *24E–25A*).

This passage implies very strongly that in the Egyptian record the location of Atlantis was uncertain and the placing of it beyond the Straits of Gibraltar was the result of discussions between Solon and the priests of Sais.

However, it seems quite clear that the Ancient Metropolis and the Royal City of Atlantis did not belong to one and the same island. The Ancient Metropolis lay on a small circular island of about 12 miles in diameter. The Royal City was on another island, rectangular in shape and much larger than the island of the Ancient Metropolis. Thus Atlantis must have consisted of at least two islands; and indeed Plato says as much:

'Now in this island of Atlantis there existed a confederation of kings of great and marvellous power, which held sway over all the island, and over many other islands also . . .' (*Tim.*, *25A*).

This, then, is what Plato says of the geographical nature and location of Atlantis; and it is remarkable enough. What he says of its date and its end is even more remarkable. In the *Critias*, Critias says at the beginning of his account of what the Egyptian priests told Solon: 'Now, first of all, we must recall the fact that 9,000 is the sum of years since the war occurred, as is recorded, between the dwellers beyond the pillars of Heracles and all that dwelt within them' (*Crit.*, *108E*), and the same figure is given in the *Timaeus* (*Tim.*, *23E*).

And in the *Timaeus*, Critias reports the speech of the Egyptian priests; after they had mentioned the resistance of the Athenians to the might of Atlantis:

'But at a later time there occurred portentous earthquakes and floods, and one grievous day and night befell them, when the whole body of your warriors was swallowed up by the earth and the island of Atlantis in like manner was swallowed up by the sea and vanished; wherefore also the ocean at that spot has now become impassable and unsearchable, being blocked up by the shoal mud which the island created as it settled down' (*Tim., 25D*).

The summary, then, of Plato's description of the physical and chronological features of Atlantis is that Atlantis consisted certainly of two islands and possibly more, and that one of these was quite small and circular and that another was roughly rectangular and immense; that it flourished at about 9600 BC; and that it sank into the sea in a day and a night.

THREE
The Dating of Plato's Atlantis

This, then, as set out in the two previous chapters, is what Plato has said about Atlantis. Is it credible? Obviously not. Can its discrepancies be reconciled? We believe they can; and we believe that the solution is both simple and conclusive. At this stage, however, the impossibilities must first be examined.

The first and most anachronistic is the date. Working back 9,000 years from the time when the Egyptian priests told Solon that Atlantis was preparing to attack Athens and Egypt and the Athenians were gallantly meeting this attack, we arrive at the approximate date of 9600 BC—a time, as Professor Marinatos has rightly said, when 'there were neither Egyptians to record the events, nor Greeks to perform the deeds attributed to them'. Neolithic remains in Lower Egypt date from about 5000 BC, the historic period beginning in the mid-Fourth Millennium BC, while Greek-speaking peoples do not appear in Greece until the Second Millennium BC.

The elaborate and developed agriculture and horticulture of Atlantis are also wildly anachronistic. The so-called 'first farmers' of Jarmo in Northern Iraq flourished around 7000 BC; and although somewhat anomalous urban cultures (which must have been based on regular agriculture) existed at Jericho and Çatal Hüyük in Anatolia at about the same period in history, the first major civilizations (which were based on agriculture)—notably the Sumerian—came into being in the Fourth Millennium BC, i.e. between 4000 and 3000 BC. Agriculture spread from the Fertile Crescent (the uplands which stretch from Persia to Syria) into Europe and Asia during the Third Millennium or a little earlier. In Denmark and Great Britain land began to be cultivated around 2500 BC; while in North America the earliest cultivation of grain appeared in New Mexico between 1500 and 1000 BC.

The inhabitants of Atlantis could read and write: their laws were *inscribed*. But the Sumerians, the world's first literate civilization, invented writing between 2700 and 2300 BC; and Egyptian hieroglyphics are perhaps somewhat earlier.

These written laws of Atlantis are inscribed on a pillar of orichalcum, an alloy of copper; and the people of Atlantis are shown as being familiar with the use and working of copper, tin, bronze, gold and silver. Now the use of the various metals began in the same way and followed the same

PLATE 1. The cloud of ash and gases thrown up by the eruption of Surtsey in 1963, at sunset. Submarine eruptions are often so violent that the cone of ejecta appears above the surface of the sea, forming a small island, as happened in the case of Surtsey. Similar eruptions created the original island of Stronghyle-Santorin, over a period of several millennia (see page 108).

sequence in all parts of the world. The use of copper came first, followed by bronze, with iron last, irrespective of the actual date of their appearance in various regions. The history of mankind falls conveniently into four ages, the Stone, the Copper (or Chalcolithic), the Bronze and the Iron Age—the names being derived from the material from which the mankind of that time made tools, weapons and other implements to serve his needs.

Gold and silver have been known for a very long time, but owing to their rarity and beauty have always been considered as precious metals—to be used for decoration and not for utility. According to the generally accepted view the use of copper and metals in general first appeared in the Middle East, among the peoples of Mesopotamia, towards the end of the Fourth Millennium BC. The Sumerians, the earliest known inhabitants of Mesopotamia, were in close touch with many regions rich in metals. From Mesopotamia the use of copper spread through Egypt, the Levant, Cyprus and the Aegean to Northern Europe and the Black Sea lands; and via the Mediterranean to Western Europe. Before the arrival of the Spaniards, North America was still in the Stone Age, although Central and Southern America had some knowledge of the use of copper and bronze; and the aborigines of Australia and New Guinea are only now emerging from their Stone Age.

The use of pure copper was restricted owing to its softness, and its influence on the development of civilization was not great. During the Copper Age stone remains the fundamental material for the tools, weapons and utensils of daily life. The age of metals really begins with the appearance of bronze. (In this connection, the term 'bronze' is used to mean the ancient alloy of approximately 90 parts of copper to 10 parts of tin, and does not mean the modern bronze which is an alloy of copper and other metals such as zinc, manganese, etc.) In regions where metals are readily available in quantity it is natural that their use should be early. In the home of metallurgy, Mesopotamia, with the abundance of copper-producing districts such as Assyria, Chaldea, etc., in Anatolia and Syria, in the ore-producing island of Cyprus, which lies on the cross-roads of Asia, Europe and Africa, the Bronze Age appears at the beginning or, at the latest, in the middle of the Third Millennium BC. In Greece, the use of bronze develops to a great degree during the Minoan and Helladic phases of the Aegean civilization, that is, between 2100 and 1200 BC. And with these figures in mind it is quite impossible, indeed absurd, to believe that the use of bronze was known in Atlantis 7,000 years earlier.

The arguments from architecture are, if not quite as neat, certainly as convincing. The earliest known examples of formal monumental architecture date from the early Fourth Millennium at Eridu in southern Mesopotamia, the earliest stone fortifications to the Seventh Millennium at Jericho, while the typical megalithic (or Cyclopean) architecture which is the closest in nature to that described for Atlantis, appearing first in Mesopotamia in the Fourth Millennium, arrived later in the

PLATE 2. Since the great eruption of *c.* 1500 BC that destroyed the centre of Santorin, minor eruptions have frequently recurred in the middle of the volcanic cavity (see page 116). The lava flow from Surtsey, shown in the photograph, recalls an eruption of Santorin in the second century BC, described by the geographer, Strabo, when 'flames rushed forth from the sea for the space of four days; causing the whole of it to boil and be all on fire; and after a little an island twelve stades in circumference, composed of the burning mass, was thrown up, as if by machinery'.

41

Aegean, Peloponnese and Crete, and reached Western Europe around 2300 BC.

There are other anachronisms which it would be wearisome to pursue since the case is already so strong. One wild anomaly could perhaps have been allowed, but for Atlantis to have everything—architecture, metallurgy, writing, agriculture and unborn opponents—between 3,000 and 7,000 years before their time is manifestly absurd. The date of 9600 BC for Atlantis is both incredible and impossible, in detail and in general alike.

Section 2

WHERE WAS ATLANTIS? OLD THEORIES DEMOLISHED

FOUR
The Atlantic Ocean

The anomaly of the date of Atlantis is at once obvious and clearcut—and, as will appear later, open to a simple solution. The other principal anomalies of the story—the very large size of Atlantis and its disappearance 'in a night and a day'—are more complex and have moreover become encrusted with so much legend, explanation and pseudo-science that a great deal of clearing and demolition work is necessary before their true shapes can be revealed.

The location of Atlantis does not seem to have troubled mankind a great deal from Plato's time until about the middle of the sixteenth century. This may be due to any or all of the following causes:

(a) The great authority of Aristotle, who considered Atlantis a myth invented by his teacher Plato.

(b) The absence of any other corroborative source contemporary with, or earlier than, Plato.

(c) The absence of scientific information which could check the size and location of Atlantis and, in particular, the date of its submersion.

Francis Bacon (1561–1626), who saw in the continent of America a 'New Atlantis'.

In spite of this and especially in spite of Aristotle's authority, Crantor, who lived in the third century BC and who was the first scholiast or commentator on Plato, believed the story to be true, as Proclus relates. According to Ammianus Marcellinus (AD 330–400), the Alexandrine scholars considered the destruction of Atlantis a historical fact. Poseidonius (135–51 BC), a Stoic philosopher and writer who travelled widely in Western Europe, believed that the Atlantis story was a combination of actual and imaginary events; and Strabo (67 BC–AD 23), the great geographer of antiquity, held the same view.

Nevertheless the great impetus for fresh speculation on the Atlantis question was provided by the discovery of America by Christopher Columbus. About sixty years after this event Francesco Lopez de Gomara (1553) expressed the view that America was the continent on the other side of the Atlantic referred to in the Platonic dialogues; and somewhat later Sir Francis Bacon put forward the hypothesis that the newly discovered continent was, in fact, Atlantis.

Atlantis, Atlantic Ocean—the solution seems obvious; and placing Atlantis in the Atlantic came as a heaven-sent answer to investigators, ancient and modern alike. The existence of a large island or continent in the waters of the Atlantic—forming a land bridge between Old and New

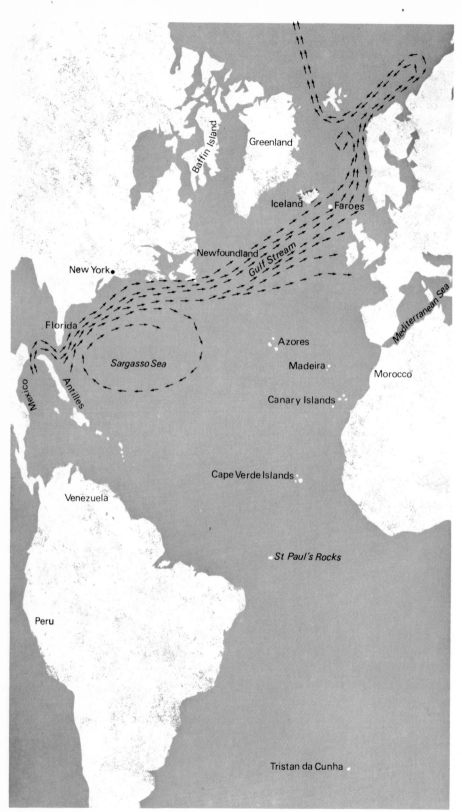

Baffin Island

Greenland

Iceland   Faroes

Newfoundland   *Gulf Stream*

New York●

Florida

Mediterranean Sea

Azores

Sargasso Sea   Madeira

Mexico   Morocco

Antilles   Canary Islands

Venezuela

Cape Verde Islands

Peru   *St Paul's Rocks*

Tristan da Cunha

Most writers on Atlantis have preferred to locate the 'lost continent' in the Atlantic Ocean. Among them was the seventeenth-century Jesuit, Athanasius Kircher, who published this map (*top right*) in his book, *Mundus Subterraneus* (1665). Another author who favoured the Atlantic as the site of Atlantis was Ignatius Donnelly, whose *Atlantis: the Antediluvian World* was published in New York in 1882 and has been one of the most influential books ever written about the legendary continent. Donnelly's 'Empire of Atlantis' included almost the whole of the ancient world, plus the Pre-Columbian civilizations of America.

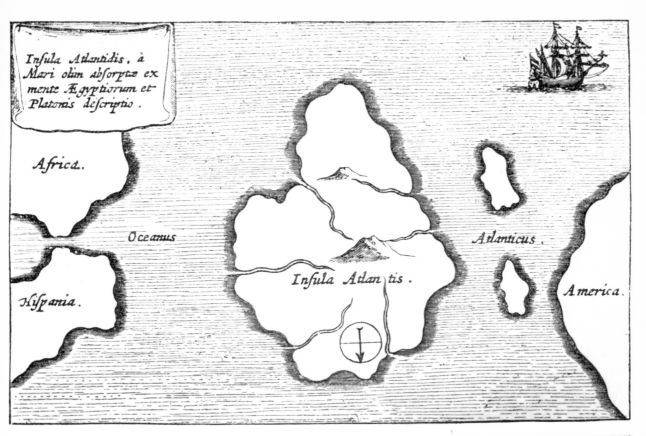

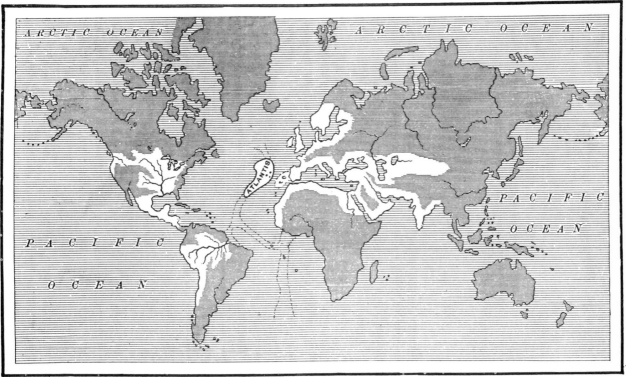

THE EMPIRE OF ATLANTIS.

The remains of the oldest North American cultures are seen by some modern writers as survivals from the civilization of Atlantis: four 'Atlanteans' from *Secret Cities of Old South America: Atlantis Unveiled*, by Harold T. Wilkins, published in London in 1950.

1 and 2.—Atlanteans (Chichen-Itza, Mayan caryatides). 3.—Bearded Atlan (later deified as rain god, ancient Mexico). 4.—Woman Atlantean (very ancient Indian glyphs, British Columbia).

Worlds—would provide a facile explanation for various similarities, geological, biological, anthropological and linguistic, which have been alleged to exist between the continents on either side of the Atlantic and their inhabitants. And it is for this reason that an Atlantic Atlantis has been supported by so many writers with such fervour, not so much in support of Plato as to provide a working hypothesis for their own theories. For such writers the question has not been whether there was indeed an island or continent of the dimensions given by Plato, but whether, in fact, there did exist a prehistoric people of such a high level of culture, the fount and origin of all later forms of civilization. Atlantis is a marvellous solution. Atlantis, such writers maintain, is the source of all the Mediterranean civilizations and those of Egypt and Mycenae and likewise of Central and South America. Atlantis, in fact, for them ranks with Ogygia, Paradise and the Garden of Eden as a symbol of the common origin of mankind and its civilizations. It is hardly necessary to point out that Plato had no such concept of Atlantis; and that the Athenians and Egyptians of his account quite clearly considered the Atlanteans enemies and aliens.

The various arguments which have been advanced in support of the former existence of Atlantis in the Atlantic Ocean may be conveniently considered (and answered) under a number of different headings.

1. The Sargasso Sea

Many writers have maintained that Atlantis stretched from the western coast of Morocco to the eastern coast of Venezuela and included the Azores, Madeira, the Canaries—and, according to some, the Cape Verde Islands, too—and the region of the Sargasso Sea.

The Sargasso Sea is the zone in the south-west of the North Atlantic

Floating masses of seaweed in the Sargasso Sea were formerly thought to indicate the presence of shallow water—the lost land of Atlantis.

COLLECTING IN THE SARGASSO SEA.

just south of the main arm of the Gulf Stream; and its name derives from the Portuguese word *sargasso*, a name for several kinds of floating seaweed. These *sargassos*, in island-like masses, cover an area of over 1,500,000 square miles (4,000,000 sq. km) or about eight times the area of France. It is said that Columbus's sailors felt great fear when they saw these 'tropical grapes' as they called them; and believed they were close to land and sailing in dangerously shallow waters. Actually at that point the Atlantic is about 3,700 fathoms (5,000 m) deep. Many of these particular seaweeds are also found attached to the rocky coasts of Australia

49

and America. For a long time their concentration, floating in this particular area of the Atlantic, appeared inexplicable; but it has now been established that they come from the coasts of Florida and are carried to the Sargasso Sea by swirling currents.

In this view of the location of Atlantis, the Azores, Madeira, the Canaries and probably the Cape Verde Islands were all mountainous parts of Atlantis, which, after the submersion of the continent, still remained above the waters like the masts of a sunken ship. And the

Bory de St Vincent published this conjectural map of Atlantis in 1803, basing it on the belief that the islands of the East Atlantic were the remains of the submerged continent.

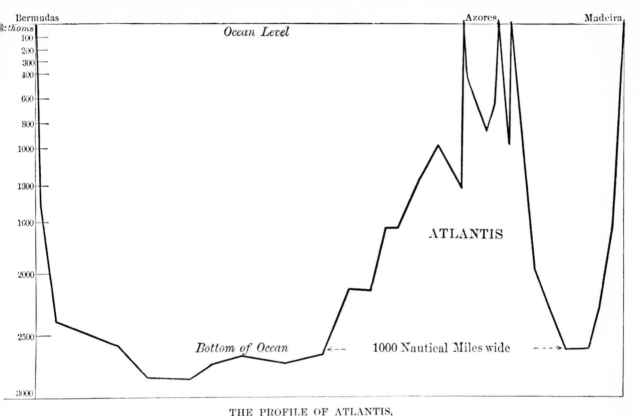

Ocean Level

ATLANTIS

Bottom of Ocean   ←--   1000 Nautical Miles wide   --→

THE PROFILE OF ATLANTIS,

As revealed by the deep-sea soundings of H. M. ship "Challenger," and the U. S. ship "Dolphin."

Deep-sea soundings in the Atlantic Ocean during the nineteenth century provided further 'proof' of the existence of the submerged continent: frontispiece from Ignatius Donnelly's *Atlantis: the Antediluvian World.*

principal arguments in support of such a large island existing in the Atlantic and simplifying communication between the Old and New Worlds are based on the retreat of the glaciers in Europe and America.

Glaciers are now restricted to the polar regions and the parts of mountains which lie above the limits of glaciation. During the Quaternary period in the Caenozoic era (i.e. between about 1,500,000 and 20,000 years ago)[1] the glaciers advanced to lower latitudes and on four consecutive occasions covered large regions of Europe and America. In Europe large masses of ice reached southwards almost to Cologne and Stalingrad and in North America to New York or St Louis, while lesser masses covered the whole of Central Europe and the mountainous parts of the Balkans as far as Greece.

There seems to be general agreement among European and American geologists that the maximum glacial advance occurred about 18,000–20,000 years ago. The retreat stage, i.e. the waning of the continental ice sheets, with minor or local re-advances, started about 19,000 years ago. Plenty of evidence shows that the shrinkage rate increased about 11,000

[1] The terms used in geological dating are relative and approximate, although generally agreed. Since they must be frequently used in this chapter, the general reader is referred to the time chart which appears on page 52.

APPROXIMATE DATES BP*	PERIODS	ERAS
11,000 - 235,000	Late Pleistocene (Monastirian)	
235,000 - 670,000	Upper Pleistocene (Tyrrhenian)	
670,000 - 1,150,000	Mid-Pleistocene (Milazzian)	
1,150,000 - 1,370,000	Lower Pleistocene (Sicilian)	
1,370,000 - 2,500,000	Early Pleistocene (Calabrian)	
Millions of years BP*		
12	Pliocene	Caenozoic
25	Miocene	
40	Oligocene	
60	Eocene	
70	Palaeocene	
135	Cretaceous	Mesozoic
180	Jurassic	
225	Triassic	
270	Permian	Palaeozoic
350	Carboniferous	
400	Devonian	
440	Silurian	
500	Ordovician	
600	Cambrian	
3,600	Pre-Cambrian	

*BP = before present day

According to Holmes (1966)

years ago and the associated rise in sea-level (from the release of frozen waters) reached approximately the present level 5,000 years ago. However, the rise to interglacial temperature levels was not completed until about 2,000–3,000 years ago. The restriction of the ice-fields to their present regions is attributed by some geologists to the warm Atlantic Ocean current; and according to these authorities this warm stream was formed after the last advance of the ice-sheets, at a time known in America as the Wisconsin Age. The appearance of the Gulf Stream is attributed to a structural change in the shape of the floor of the Atlantic Ocean owing to tectonic accidents of earth-movement during that period. According to the supporters of the absolute veracity of Plato's story as it was written, the submersion of Atlantis was one of the most decisive of geotectonic events, and they claim that a strong argument in their favour is the close coincidence of the dates of the retreat of the glaciers from Europe and North America with the date which Plato gives for the submersion of Atlantis, i.e. 9,000 years before Solon's visit to Egypt, or about 9600 BC. And this theory, it will be noted, puts the birth of the Gulf Stream at the same date, about 9600 BC.

2. The Atlantic Land Bridge

A view held in some quarters is that there existed a bridge of land across the Atlantic Ocean, joining America with Europe and Africa until the middle of the Cretaceous period. This bridge would have divided the Atlantic into two smaller basins. At the end of the Cretaceous or the beginning of the Tertiary, this bridge, it is maintained, would have disappeared as a result of downward epeirogenic (or continent-making) movements of the earth's crust, thus creating the Atlantic Ocean in its present form. At the same time, i.e. some 60,000,000 years ago, the Gulf Stream would have come into existence.

3. The Mid-Atlantic Ridge

Another argument to which adherents of the location of Atlantis in the Atlantic Ocean have appealed is the existence of the Mid-Atlantic Ridge. But this ridge, which for the greater part is covered by water to a depth of 1,600 fathoms (3,000 m) is not the result of a submersion of a piece of land. On the contrary, this ridge, which extends in an S-shape from north to south, from Iceland past St Paul's Rocks to Tristan da Cunha and beyond, was formed by the rising of the ocean floor under the influence of orogenic (or mountain-making) movements in that area. It is much longer and broader than the Alpine–Himalayan mountain systems and is structurally connected with the East African Rift Valley system. It continues, moreover, round the Cape of Good Hope and joins the central ridge in the Indian Ocean, the two ridges belonging to the tectonic complex which surrounds the African block. The length of the Central Indo-Atlantic

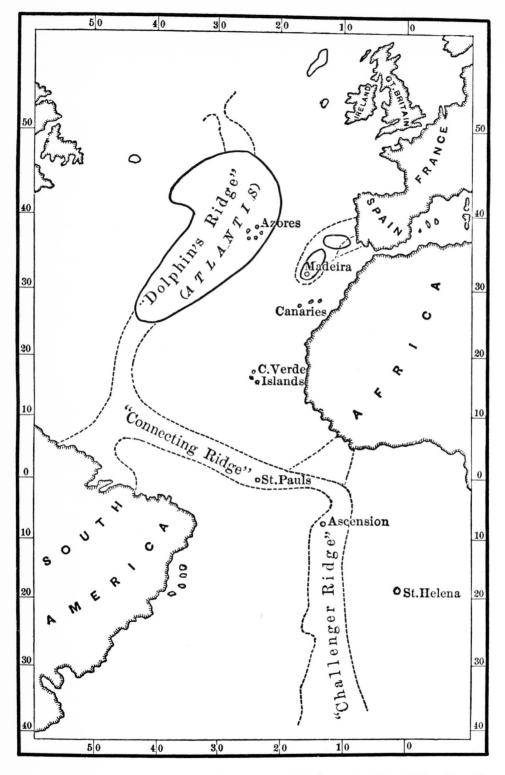

MAP OF ATLANTIS, WITH ITS ISLANDS AND CONNECTING RIDGES, FROM DEEP-SEA
SOUNDINGS.

Those who believed that Atlantis was in the Atlantic Ocean were encouraged by the discovery in the nineteenth century of the Mid-Atlantic Ridge, a huge submarine mountain range running roughly north–south along the ocean floor: the map on the opposite page is from Donnelly's *Atlantis: the Antediluvian World*. It is now known that the Mid-Atlantic Ridge is not an isolated phenomenon, but is part of a belt of sub-oceanic ridges that extend well beyond the Atlantic Ocean.

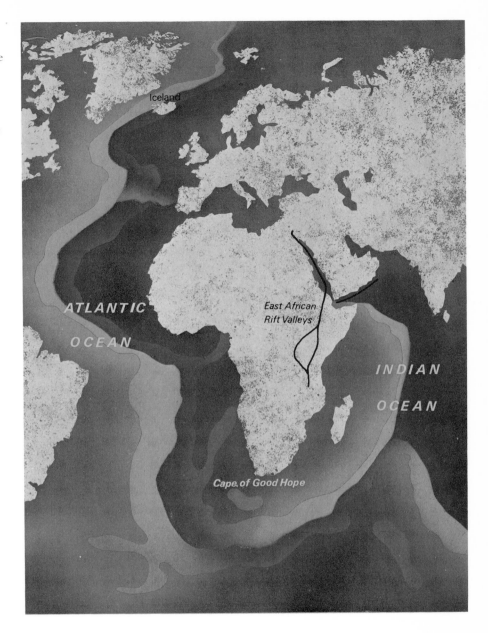

seismic (or earthquake) zone is more than 18,600 miles (30,000 km). Recent research has shown conclusively that the Mid-Atlantic Ridge belongs to a world-encircling morpho-tectonic belt 40,000 miles long, passing through the Indian and South Pacific Oceans, the Norwegian Sea and the Arctic Basin. Furthermore, there is a considerable body of evidence that the limits of the Mid-Atlantic Ridge have not changed significantly since, at least, the Middle Eocene time.

Helium age-measurements of fragments of basalt taken from the area where Atlantis is supposed to have been (Lat. 30°01′ N, Long. 45°01′ W) have confirmed volcanic activity on the ocean floor in Tertiary times and showed that the Mid-Atlantic Ridge was formed at least 15 million years ago. Similarly, from the thickness of the sedimentary rocks in the middle of the Atlantic at Lat. 34°57′ N, Long. 44°16′ W, it has been estimated that that area has been the floor of the sea for at least 280,000 years. Again, measurements by the ionium method of specimens found 812 miles (1,300 km) east of Newfoundland showed that the Mid-Atlantic Ridge there had been the floor of the sea for the past 72,500 years. Finally, radiocarbon dating of deep-sea sediment cores from various places in the Atlantic has established that these sediments were deposited about 30,000 years ago.

Such measurements, therefore, and other oceanographic research afford clear proof that the Atlantic Ocean existed in its present form long before the decay of the ice-sheets; and the sedimentary basins remained tectonically quiet (i.e. suffered no major change) during the whole time required to deposit the sedimentary sequence.

As regards the suggestion that the retreat of the glaciers was caused by the warm Gulf Stream: the writers who claim that Atlantis was situated in the Atlantic Ocean contend, as we have seen, that the Gulf Stream was brought into existence by the subsidence of the island of Atlantis some 11,500 years ago. But there is considerable evidence that the Gulf Stream existed at least before the end of the Cretaceous era, i.e. 60 million years ago. The examination of forty-one deep-sea sediment cores taken from various places in the Atlantic has proved the existence of pre-Pleistocene sediments across the whole breadth of the ocean. The oldest sediment found is Upper Cretaceous in date; and the absence of sediments of older than Late Cretaceous and the restricted thickness of unconsolidate sediment (2,600–3,300 ft or 800–1,000 m) – as measured by seismic methods – together suggest that a large-scale reorganization of the Atlantic Basin took place at some time during the latter part of the Mesozoic era. As indicated by the widespread appearance of marine deposits on both sides of the Atlantic in Aptian–Albian times, the reorganization of the Atlantic Basin was completed 120,000,000 years ago – long before man appeared on the earth.

The evidence of the Atlantic sediments is conclusive. Radiocarbon dating of pelagic and abyssal sediment cores[1] shows that the rate of deposition (i.e. the building up of these sediments) in the Atlantic during the Pleistocene period was between 10 and 20 cm per 1,000 years. During the Ice Ages this deposition rate rose to 60 cm per 1,000 years; while since the Ice Ages, the rate is computed at 3–10 cm per 1,000 years. So if the Atlantic Ocean had been formed 11,000 years ago (i.e. with the supposed submersion of Atlantis in 9500 BC) the thickness of the deposits would not have much exceeded one metre (i.e. 11 × 10 cm). Even if the rate of sedimentation was equal to the highest estimated during the glacial age (i.e. 11 × 60 cm) it still would only have been about 6·5 metres, and, with

---

[1] These cores are obtained by driving a hollow drill into the ocean sediments, in the same way as oil-men drill into the earth. The resultant core, rather like the specimen obtained by a cheese-tasting tool, can be scientifically examined and analysed.

PLATE 3. Relief model of Santorin, made in Athens more than forty years ago on the basis of the British Admiralty chart of 1916. The steep sides of the caldera created by the tremendous eruption can be clearly seen.

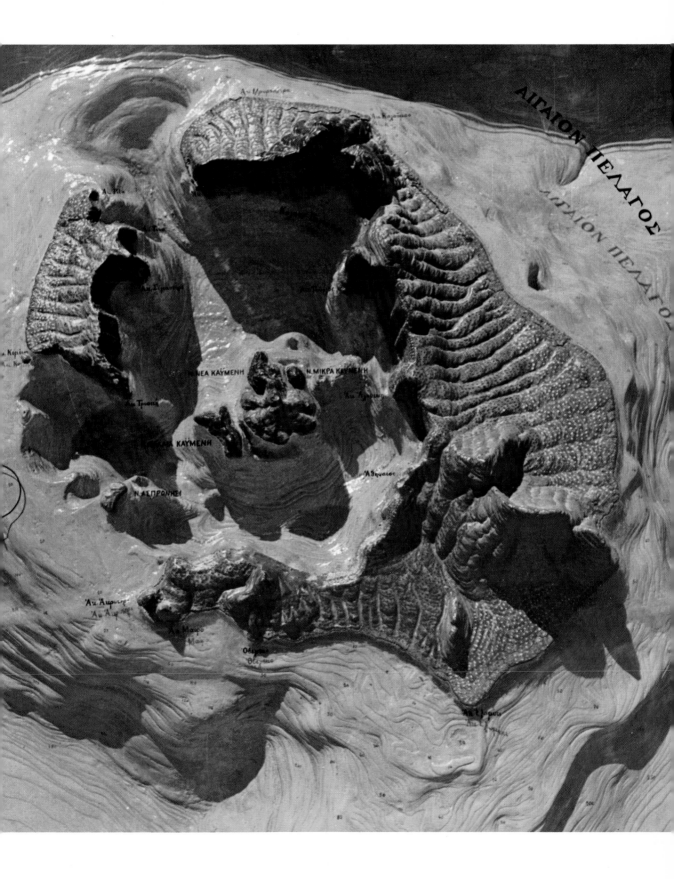

modern methods of exploring the deep-sea floor, finding remains of buildings and structures under such a thin layer of sediment would not be a very difficult matter. Unfortunately for this supposition, however, the actual thickness of the deposits in the Atlantic exceeds 2,600 ft, or 800 metres.

Further, although the proposition that the Gulf Stream came into existence after the last Ice Age would explain the retreat of the last glaciation, it would not explain satisfactorily why the ice retreated at the end of the previous Ice Ages. Palaeoclimatological research has shown that similar changes of climate, though on a considerably smaller scale, have taken place in the past 60,000–80,000 years. The climatic changes during the Pleistocene era were marked by five temperature maxima of the same order as the present climate; and these observations lead us to believe that an internal self-regulating mechanism controlled the climatic changes during the Pleistocene period.

That the alternations of glacial and interglacial stages did not require external influences (such as the Gulf Stream) or catastrophic events (such as the subsidence of Atlantis) to initiate or maintain them is shown by a most ingenious and revolutionary theory put forward by the geophysicists Maurice Ewing and William Donn of Columbia University.

From palaeoclimatic evidence it is deduced that at the beginning of the Cambrian Period (600 million years ago) the North Pole was in the North Pacific Ocean but that it reached the Arctic Ocean during the Tertiary Period. This sudden movement of the Pole is attributed to convection currents, and these currents, or perhaps some other mechanism, caused the outer layers of the earth's crust to slip over the inner layers of the earth. While the Pole was in the Pacific, currents from southern latitudes would pass over it and warm it and, in consequence, the whole climate of the earth would be warmer. But when the North Pole migrated to the Arctic Ocean, the polar region would be almost totally cut off from the warm currents of the Pacific. Moreover the flow of warm water from the Atlantic would be comparatively small, owing to the series of submarine rises or sills represented by the line Scotland–Faröes–Iceland–Greenland and the Canadian Archipelago which intervenes between the Atlantic and Arctic Oceans.

At the start of the first Ice Age about 1,500,000 years ago (i.e. the time when the North Pole moved to its Arctic Ocean location) the sea level was relatively high. This being so, the waters of the Atlantic could flow freely over the submarine sills which divide the Arctic from the Atlantic. In the cold Arctic Ocean area the warm water coming from the south evaporated in vast amounts and was transformed into snow. The snowfall over the northern continents covered them in a sheet of ice. But since in this way a large quantity of water was, as it were, withdrawn from circulation, the sea level fell. As a result, the warm water from the Atlantic ceased passing over the submarine sills in sufficient quantity to reach and melt the Arctic Ocean. The Arctic Ocean froze, evaporation ceased and

PLATE 4. The cliffs of the Santorin caldera, looking north from the town of Phera, with Cape Oea in the distance.

57

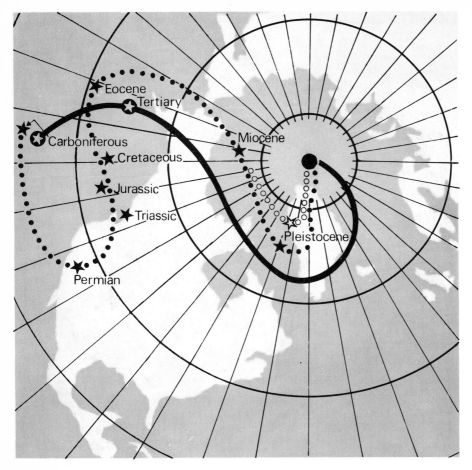

Alternative paths of the North Pole at different periods of geological history, from palaeoclimatic and palaeo-magnetic evidence. The migration of the Pole provides a theory of the Ice Ages without postulating the submersion of Atlantis.

so did the snowfall. Without a steady supply of snow the glaciers began to diminish and the Ice Age came to an end.

According to a recent modification of this theory, at a time of glacial culmination the temperature of ocean surface waters would be lowered sufficiently to decrease the rate of evaporation and hence that of the precipitation over the ice sheets; then through the combined effects of decreased nourishment and increased warming of the margin of the ice sheets, due to the small albedo of water (i.e. the high absorption of the radiation received by the North Atlantic surface water), the ice sheets would retreat.

In either case, as the glaciers waned, so the sea level again rose. Warm water from the Atlantic began again to flow freely over the sills in sufficient quantities to affect and melt the Arctic Ocean. Evaporation began once more, snowfall followed and so, inevitably, a new Ice Age began.

So, in accordance with the geophysical mechanism, glaciation in the Northern Hemisphere is initiated by an increase in precipitation and terminated by a decrease in precipitation. There is evidence that the polar ice-pack is again melting owing to a small increase in ocean-heat flux resulting from the post-glacial rise in sea level, or, possibly, from a small increase in radiation. The world's temperature today is the maximum recorded during an interglacial period. Therefore, if the North Pole retains its present position, a fall of temperature and a new Ice Age may be expected – in a few thousand years' time.

4. The argument of the vitreous lava

In 1898 a ship laying an Atlantic cable drew up from the ocean floor 560 miles (900 km) north of the Azores at Lat. 47°00 N, Long. 27°20′ W, at a depth of 1,640 fathoms (3,000 m), a piece of tachylite, which is basaltic lava with a vitreous texture. This specimen is now at the Ecole des Mines in Paris. If the lava had been formed on the ocean floor under the pressure of 3,000 metres of water, it would have had a crystalline and not a vitreous texture. That being so, P. Termier examined the specimen and concluded that the lava had been consolidated under normal atmospheric pressure. Therefore, it was argued that the region between the Azores and Iceland was still land when the lava was ejected and that later this land subsided to a depth of 3,000 metres and formed the floor of the Atlantic Ocean.

Now the validity of this argument depends on whether or not this specimen of tachylite was formed in the place where it was found. It could, however, equally well have been ice-rafted (i.e. carried to that point on floating ice) or carried to its final position from neighbouring volcanic islands by means of turbidity currents. A turbidity current is a kind of high-density current flowing on the sea floor just as mercury flows beneath water; and its high density is due to sediment in turbulent suspension. Modern research has shown that terrestrial organic remains, as well as wood and the leaves of trees, are often carried along by such turbidity currents and deposited in the submarine canyons of the Magdalena and Congo rivers. Grass, still green, was discovered in 1935 at a depth of 750 fathoms, 12 miles out to sea from the estuary of the Magdalena (in the Gulf of California); while the Congo carries fresh-water diatoms hundreds of miles out to sea. The latter have indeed been found in a core from the crest of the Mid-Oceanic Ridge near the equator. R. Malaise supported the view that these diatoms were deposited in small lakes when the Mid-Oceanic Ridge was land. Bruce Heezen and M. Tharp, however, mention 'that (1) the layer of fresh water diatoms is approximately a millimetre thick, interbedded with typical deep-sea sediments and (2) the winds blowing off Africa often carry such large quantities of diatom testas[1] as to lay down layers of appreciable thickness on the decks of ships'. In addition, of course, surface currents could have carried the diatoms found on the Mid-Oceanic Ridge. Again, at 4,850 fathoms in the Puerto Rico Trench, fragments of the alga *Halimeda* were found; and living *Halimeda* requires sunlight. According to the prevailing view these fragments came from the land and were carried to the position in which they were found by

[1]The testa is the flinty coat or shell which is all that survives of diatoms, a form of microscopic alga.

59

turbidity currents. On these grounds, therefore, it is probable that a piece of tachylite was carried to the position in which it was found by surface or bottom currents. The position of individual rocks can be explained in various ways. A. S. Laughton, for example, writing recently (1967), states: 'More frequently loose boulders are recovered from scree slopes and weathered outcrops. This means that there is always doubt whether the rocks are representative of the local outcrop or have been brought from afar by ice rafting, tree root rafting and other less important means. In the North Atlantic, ice-rafted erratics are known to comprise more than 50 per cent of many rock collections.' And in support of the possibility of ice-rafting, cores taken between 40° and 50° N in the north and north-western North Atlantic have been reported to contain black pumice and brown and black glass, probably derived from near Iceland and carried to their position by ice-rafting.

But even if one is not inclined to accept the view that the specimen of lava found on the bottom of the Atlantic was ice-rafted to that position or carried by turbidity currents, still the presence there of vitreous lava by no means indicates that the place where it was deposited was dry land which subsided at the end of the last Ice Age. The Mid-Atlantic Expedition of 1947 dredged basalt boulders from the crestal area of the Mid-Atlantic Ridge near 30° N, and these boulders were covered with layers of dark-brown, vesicular, basaltic glass; and recent research has shown that Lower Miocene microfossils occur in the basaltic glass. A basalt dredged from the crest of the Mid-Atlantic Ridge at 45° N has been dated by the potassium–argon technique to 29 ± 4 million years old. Furthermore, the sedimentation history of the Atlantic shows that the unconsolidated sediments over the Mid-Atlantic Ridge, at least between 30° N and 29° S, have been entirely deposited since the early Miocene.

The rate of erosion or alteration of the sea floor cannot give any indication of dating. As is known, more than 15,000 years are required for lava to be altered. Furthermore it is likely that a layer of volcanic tuff or ash would have covered the lava before it became the sea floor; and in such a case the presence of the superficial layer of ash would prevent the erosion of the lava until the superficial layer itself had been eroded or washed away by submarine currents.

All things considered, it seems most likely that the lava found in the Atlantic came from a submarine volcano whose cone briefly rose above the surface of the sea. Submarine eruptions are often so violent that the materials thrown out form small volcanic islands – as has been seen recently near Iceland (plates 1, 2, 21). Owing to the looseness of the ejecta of which they are made, coupled with the destructive action of the ocean waves, these islands usually disappear after a short while.

The history of volcanic regions is full of such examples. Five such are recorded in the volcanic history of the Azores. After a submarine eruption between Sao Miguel and Terceira (the outermost of the Azores) on 31 December 1719, a new island came into existence, which then disappeared in 1723. Another eruption between Terceira and Graciosa was recorded on 1 June 1867; and the volcanic cone formed by it shortly afterwards subsided into the ocean depths. A submarine eruption on 1 February 1871 off the west coast of Sao Miguel produced another short-lived island; and yet another was formed and disappeared $5\frac{1}{2}$ miles (9 km) south of Sao Jorge in July 1880. The most interesting case, however, occurred much more recently—on 28 September 1957. In this case a submarine eruption half a mile off the west coast of Fajal—the northernmost of the Azores— led to the formation of a new island with an area of 6 sq. km. It is reported that fragments of lava reached a height of 2,300 ft (700 m); and by 14 October a small round island 730 yds (700 m) in diameter had been formed, standing 330 ft (100 m) above sea level. After twenty days this island disappeared again into the depths of the sea.

Now, the contours of the Atlantic floor show that the tachylite specimens, which are the source of this particular theory, were raised from the rift valley in the Mid-Atlantic Ridge. Taking into consideration the form of the sea floor and the volcanic history of the Azores region, it is therefore most likely that the tachylite specimens from the sea originated from a volcanic island of temporary existence or are volcanic extrusion material carried along the rift valley by sea currents from the Azores plateau.

5. The argument of the East Atlantic Continent

J. F. Rothé has advanced the opinion that the eastern section of the Atlantic Ocean has a continental structure; and so the proponents of an Atlantic Atlantis suggest that this supposedly submerged continent could have been the location of Atlantis. Rothé's opinions have not been accepted. The layer which lies under the unconsolidated sediment in this area and which has the characteristics of the continental granite layer is shown by seismic measurements in the Atlantic Ocean to be considerably less thick than the granitic layer under the continents. On the continents the earth's crust consists of a layer of sialic rocks (silicate of aluminium) of a thickness of the order of 6·2 miles (10 km) with small variations from place to place. At Lat. 53°50′ N, Long. 18°40′ W, the thickness of the sialic rocks under the Atlantic does not exceed 1·9 miles (3 km) according to investigations made by an expedition sponsored by the University of Cambridge.

If the eastern section of the Atlantic had been formed by the submersion of land extending between the African block and the Mid-Atlantic Ridge, the thickness of the earth's crust in that region should have been at least equal to the average thickness of the crust under the continents. This crust thickness varies between 19 and 44 miles (30 and 70 km); and the maximum known depth of the Mohorovičić discontinuity, 37–44 miles (60–70 km), is in the European Southern Alps and the Sierra Nevada, California. The Mohorovičić discontinuity is a surface of discontinuity which separates the earth's crust from the underlying layer known as the

Mantle. Under mountainous regions of moderate height the Mohovoričić discontinuity is generally at a depth of 31 miles (50 km) while in lowlands near the ocean shores it is at a depth of about 22 miles (35 km).

Now, according to Plato's description, Atlantis was famous for the high mountains surrounding the great plain. If Atlantis lay in the Atlantic Ocean the thickness of the earth's crust under the ocean floor in that region should have been over 22 miles (35 km); but in the Indian and Atlantic Oceans the thickness of the crust from the sea hardly reaches 12–19 miles (20–30 km).

Further, a comparison of geophysical results obtained at sea with those obtained on land shows that there is a basic difference between the structure of oceans and that of continents. Many hundreds of gravity observations show that the average value of gravity over the deep oceans is, without exception, 300 or 400 milligals above what would be expected if the ocean floor were a depressed continent covered by water. According to Sir Edward Bullard 'the deep ocean basins can never have been parts of continents'.

Finally, even if we accept the hypothesis that the eastern section of the Atlantic Ocean originated from a submersion of land, this event could not have occurred at the end of the last Ice Age. As previously mentioned, all over the Atlantic Ocean floor there are unconsolidated sediments of pre-Pleistocene date. From the pattern of distribution of sediment thickness, particularly as regards the gradual increase in thickness towards the continents, Bruce C. Heezen and Marie Tharp were led to conclude 'that land connections across the deep basins of the Atlantic have not existed in the form of sunken continents, isthmian links or closely-spaced insular "stepping-stones"'. Consequently the Atlantic Ocean must have existed in its present form for at least a million years.

6. The argument from submarine river-beds and canyons

If Atlantis was submerged in the Atlantic Ocean the shores of the continents bordering on the Atlantic must have broken off to some degree and subsided into the sea. Now those who believe in this theory point out that the eroding capability of rivers (i.e. their power of carving out a channel) stops when they enter the ocean because fresh water is lighter than sea water and therefore remains on the surface. For this reason the existence of submarine beds of rivers flowing into the Atlantic has been considered as proof that Atlantis was situated in what is now the Atlantic Ocean.

There are, in fact, deep furrows on the ocean floor, the extensions of the beds of rivers flowing into the Atlantic; and these furrows extend to a great distance from the shore, reaching a depth of about 1,600 fathoms (3,000 m). A classic example is that of the Hudson River, which flows from New York. Its river bed continues under water in the form of a deep canyon to a depth of 1,100 fathoms (2,000 m). The sides of this canyon are steep and more than 330 ft (100 m) high. Near the deepest parts of

The extension of the Hudson river valley across the bed of the Atlantic Ocean is a typical submarine canyon; it was formed several million years ago and does not constitute evidence of the submerged island of Atlantis.

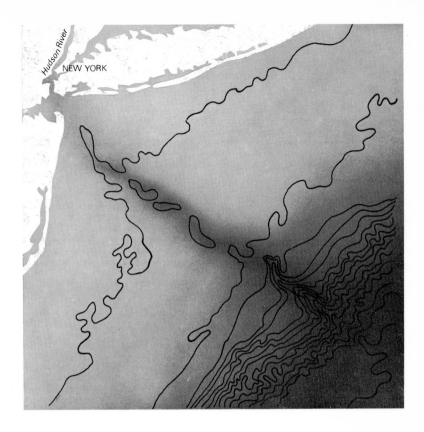

the ocean, the beds of tributaries join this submarine canyon which has been traced to a depth of 1,400 fathoms (2,700 m). The writers who support the theory that Atlantis was submerged in the Atlantic believe that the shape of the ocean floor points to the fact that the river beds were formed on land and later submerged. But according to prevailing views only the Congo and Indus submarine canyons are connected with the continental river systems; canyons in submarine slopes like that of the Hudson are a common occurrence in the oceans, and, according to Francis P. Shepard, 'In whatever way they were formed . . . they are not a recent product, but have been in existence for millions of years.'

The proponents of this theory also point to a subsidence of the Atlantic coasts on the shores of the northern countries of Europe where the submersion dates from the time of the retreat of the glaciers. The separation of the British Isles from the continental mainland and the submersion of the Norwegian coasts are attributed to similar subsidences which occurred at that period. But the supporters of this theory forget that before the waning of the ice sheets the level of the sea was 55 fathoms (100 m) lower than at present; and the English Channel and, for that matter, the Bering Strait were dry land during the Ice Age. At that same period the area covered by the Atlantic Ocean was much smaller owing to the lower sea level. The submarine river beds, now 55 fathoms (100 m) deep, were on dry land during the Ice Age, but when the ice melted the sea level rose

and these regions were slowly covered by the sea. These regions did not sink; they were simply inundated by what are called eustatic changes of the sea level.

These eustatic changes are sea level fluctuations produced on a large scale over long periods of time. Such changes have occurred in the past chiefly owing to the formation or melting of continental ice sheets during the glacial or post-glacial periods.

According to Ericson and his collaborators the Hudson submarine canyon (which extends to a depth of 1,600 fathoms (3,000 m)) was formed by the erosion of the ocean floor by turbidity currents. The largest deep-sea natural levees (embankments flanking submarine river beds) which have been observed to date are those of the Congo Canyon, which at a depth of 2,250 fathoms are 100 fathoms high and over 20 miles (32 km) wide. The natural levees of the Congo Canyon and of the Northwest Atlantic Mid-Ocean Canyon, according to the prevailing view, are the sides of tilted fault blocks carved out by turbidity currents.

In general, the large submarine canyons are fault-bounded rift valleys, eroded and scoured by underwater currents. The shaping of the ocean floor by turbidity currents is a universal phenomenon found in all oceans and the erosion by bottom currents is similar to that produced by wind and water on land, but smaller in extent. Even ripple marks which for long had been considered to be exclusively surface water formations and

Ripple marks on the deep-sea floor have been thought by some Atlantis theorists to be evidence of water formerly shallow; in fact, they are formed by turbidity currents at considerable depths and have been observed in water as deep as 2,000 fathoms. The photograph shows sand and half-submerged rocks in an area approximately four feet by seven; it was taken at a depth of 1,710 fathoms.

an irrefutable proof of shallow water deposits have now been observed at a depth of 2,000 fathoms. Furthermore deep-sea dunes, produced by strong bottom-scour, have been observed at a depth of 2,400 fathoms.

7. The argument from the nuptial migration of eels

This theory is a somewhat fanciful interpretation of what Professor Koumaris has called the 'macabre honeymoon' of the freshwater eel. When freshwater eels reach the reproductive stage they come down to the sea and swim out into the Atlantic, the European eels westwards, the American eels eastwards. It has been generally believed that all European and American eels, even those living in marshes, make their way, even sometimes over dry land, via the Atlantic to the Sargasso Sea, especially the central part. There, after laying their eggs in the seaweed at a depth of about 160 fathoms (300 m) the male and female eels die. Thereafter a proportion of the young eels (at this stage called leptocephali) which hatch out between March and July return to America, taking one year for the journey, while another proportion of the total is carried by the Gulf Stream to Europe. The leptocephali which are carried towards Europe form shoals about 75 ft (25 m) thick and 300 ft (90 m) wide; and during a long stay in the sea begin their transformation, becoming small transparent eels and slowly changing colour, first to green and finally to grey.

The transformations they undergo depend on the length of their stay in the sea. The leptocephali which go to America remain in the sea for a year at most, while those which are carried to Europe are in the sea for two or three years. Because of this the Europe-bound leptocephali undergo more transformations, and in this way a different subspecies of eels is produced. This subspecies was considered a new and distinct species, and in order to explain the difference it was supposed that the leptocephali hatched from the eggs of European eels returned to Europe while the leptocephali of American parentage went to America.

This assumption, a quite simple one, was believed to require an explanation; and Atlantis was again called upon to provide it. The proponents of the Atlantic Atlantis believe that eels formerly lived in the fresh waters of Atlantis. The great river of Atlantis, they suppose, issued into a region now occupied by the Sargasso Sea. At the delta of this river a colossal marsh is imagined to have existed—an ideal breeding-place, one might imagine, for eels. So at their season of reproduction, the eels of Atlantis simply swam down the river and laid their eggs in the swamp. Then, after the submersion of Atlantis and the disappearance of the great prehistoric river, the eels, so the argument goes, took refuge in the continents on either side of the ocean. But since then, as those continents do not afford suitable breeding grounds, the eels, guided by an age-old instinct, migrate for breeding purposes to the place where their distant progenitors were hatched.

However, it has recently been suggested that the European eels never reach the Sargasso Sea at all. If they did so, it is claimed, they would have been fished across the whole breadth of the Atlantic—but this does not occur. Hence one modern view is that all the European eels perish on the way and never reach the Sargasso Sea and that all the young eels which come to Europe are the offspring of American eels. Consequently no amount of intensive fishing of European eels could cause the extinction of the species. This view is, however, rejected by Bruun, and the matter is in dispute.

Another argument considered irrefutable by the supporters of Atlantis-in-the-Atlantic is the existence of an insect in the Sargasso Sea which moves over the water and crosses from one bunch of seaweed to another. But modern research has shown that there exist exclusively marine insects apart from those which live on sea-shores and take refuge in rock-crevices or subsoil when high tide approaches. The Sargasso species is not remarkable and is classified with the *Halobates* or 'water-bugs', which live in and move over the surfaces of marshes and rivers. There are in fact more than 40 species of *Halobates* living on warm seas.

Finally, even if we accept the view that European eels travel to the Sargasso Sea to lay their eggs and die, and that their descendants return to Europe, guided by a hereditary instinct, it does not follow that this instinct should necessarily be dated from the time of the last Ice Age; and it would be no more extravagant to assume that such an instinct dated from older geological times. But, as can be shown conclusively, the existence of a land bridge across the Atlantic during Tertiary times is geologically impossible.

8. The common flora and fauna argument

The existence of various species of plants and animals common to both sides of the Atlantic, the Mediterranean basin, the Azores, Madeira, the Canaries, the Antilles and Central America has been held to indicate that Europe and North America once had a land connection; and, naturally, those who support the theory that Atlantis was in the Atlantic believe that this link took the form of a land bridge across the Atlantic. Theoretically, of course, this link could take the form of any land connection between Eurasia and North America. In many cases, moreover, the similarities in plants and animals could have occurred without the continents ever having been joined; and this is especially the case where birds and plants are concerned. The seeds of many plants are carried for great distances by the wind—and birds fly. Floating pieces of wood are carried many miles by ocean currents and such pieces of wood can carry seeds or small animals on them. Migratory birds constantly cross great stretches of ocean.

It is often difficult to discriminate between a natural migration or colonization and a spread due to the influence of man. We are, of course, certain that the horse as we know it did not exist in America before the arrival there of the Spaniards; and conversely the agave and the prickly pear which are so common in the Mediterranean reached Europe only after the discovery of America. The same, however, cannot be said about many genera of plants, such as birch, hazel, oak, pine, etc., which flourish in Canada as well as in northern Europe. If these plants were of the same species the connection between Europe and America must have existed in late geological times. If, however, the land link between America and Europe existed only during earlier geological times, the evolution of forms in common must have differed on either side of the Atlantic. A close examination has shown that the flora on each side of the ocean have many common genera but that there is only a very small number of autochthonous species which are the same on both sides; and this limited number of common species is evidence that there was no land bridge during the later geological times and particularly during the Quaternary Period, i.e. the last 1,500,000 years.

If there had been a land bridge during the Quaternary Period, the number of species common to both sides would have been much greater. Yet a species such as the mammoth which existed in the Ice Age in Siberia is met with in America only very occasionally, while the rhinoceros of the Glacial period, although very common in Europe, is not found among the ancient fauna of North America.

During the Tertiary Period (1,500,000–64,000,000 years ago) the sequoia (or redwood) was widely spread in Europe, but it does not appear at all in the glacial period, and today is found only as a planted exotic in European parks and gardens. In America it is wild only in the coastal ranges of California. The swamp cypress (*Taxodium*) is another example of a tree which existed on both sides of the Atlantic during the Tertiary; today the genus is met with only in northern and central America. The pineapple, today a purely American plant, grew in the Rhine valley during the Tertiary. The main stem of the horse family was evolved in North America, where the modern genus *Equus* emerged in the late Tertiary. It migrated from America to Asia and, curiously enough, vanished from the land of its origin.

Returning to the question of a hypothetical land bridge, it has already been mentioned that if a continent subsided to oceanic depths (more than 4,000 m) one would expect the crustal structure to be markedly different in that area from the crustal structure in other oceanic areas. On the other hand, the fact that flat-topped submarine mountains (or *guyots*) are relatively few in the Atlantic lends no support to the view that a 'stepping stone' type of land bridge ever existed across the deep sea. Botanists, moreover, maintain that small islands would not develop a continental type of vegetation and so would not act as a land bridge.

Had a land bridge or string of 'stepping stone' islands existed joining Europe and North America, the most probable location for it would have been in the Iceland–Greenland region. Greenland is the largest island in the world. Iceland is the biggest island in the Atlantic and at the same

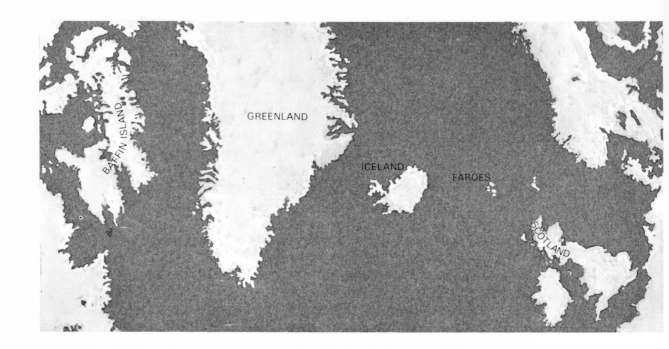

time the world's largest volcanic island, its volcanic history going back to the Tertiary when it was already dry land. There is, however, no geological evidence that Iceland was joined to Europe through the Faröes during the Tertiary and Quaternary Periods; and it may be added that the absence of wild land animals in the Icelandic plateau, together with the character of the flora, argues against any connection with either Europe or America at the time of the building of the Tertiary plateau. During the Ice Ages the area of the islands of Greenland, Iceland and the Faröes was certainly larger than it is today, but a continuous land bridge formed by these islands between Europe and America could not have been made simply as a result of the eustatic lowering of the sea level.

The distances are as follows: between Scotland and the Faröes, 190 miles (300 km); between the Faröes and Iceland 250 miles (400 km); between Iceland and Greenland, 190 miles (300 km); and between Greenland and Baffin Land 310 miles (500 km). And the depth of sea between these various points varies between 130 and 270 fathoms (250 and 500 m).

Now, according to Bruce C. Heezen and Marie Tharp, if a nearly continuous land bridge between Europe and Iceland is required it must be assumed that the Iceland–Faröes Ridge has subsided more than 200 m in the last 200,000 years. 'Current estimates of the maximum Pleistocene lowering of sea level do not exceed 160 m; thus, even if the maximum lowering of sea level during penultimate glaciation were 40 m greater than current estimates, the Faröes–Iceland–Greenland Ridge would not provide a continuous land bridge from Europe to Iceland and Greenland.' On the other hand, the depth of the sea at the Bering Strait does

The chain of islands across the North Atlantic, of which the largest are Greenland, Iceland, and the British Isles, has sometimes been thought to represent the remains of a land bridge from Europe to North America. It is almost certainly nothing of the kind.

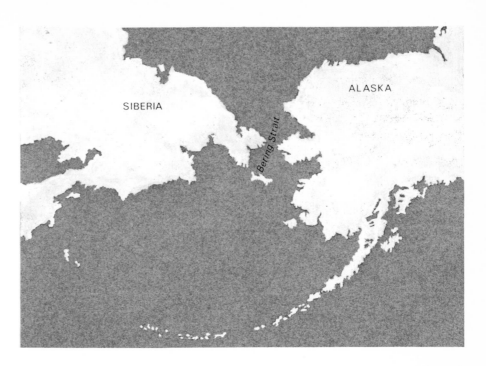

SIBERIA

ALASKA

Bering Strait

A land bridge across what is now the Bering Strait existed some 20,000 years ago.

not exceed 25-30 fathoms (50-60 m) and the width of the strait is only 46 miles (75 km). Thus the joining of Eurasia with America during the glacial period was more probably accomplished across the Bering Strait. During the Ice Age, the sea-level was at least 55 fathoms (100 m) lower and in consequence the Bering Strait was dry land. Owing to the relatively short interval of time covered by the Late Pleistocene, we should exclude the possibility of large tectonic changes in the absolute elevation of the Iceland–Greenland Ridge.

This ridge might have been a land bridge or bridge of islands, but only during pre-Tertiary times, i.e. more than 60,000,000 years ago. If a land bridge is required to explain the few genera common to America and Eurasia, the obvious position is at the Bering Strait.

9. The argument from cultural similarities

This argument has much in common with the last, though less validity, and it can be dealt with in much the same fashion.

A comparison of the arts and crafts of ancient peoples who lived in or near the Mediterranean basin with those of the Americas might lead one to suppose that the cultures of the two worlds showed some curious analogies. According to Dévigné, the two hemispheres were inhabited by people of the same race—'the Copper Race'. This race, it is claimed, appears on both sides of the Atlantic wherever copper is found, from Barbary (Morocco) to Egypt and Chaldaea, the Etruscan regions in Italy, the Basque country in Spain and France, the Canary Isles and also in Central and South America from Mexico to Peru. The peoples of this race

69

are alleged to have had the same skin colour (brown to red), the same institutions, inclinations and customs such as embalming the dead, the same symbols including the cross, the same religion involving sun-worship, educated priests especially proficient in astronomy, human sacrifice and the common feature of building trapezoidal temples of megaliths covered with gold plate. They are also pictured as having had the same traditions and crafts such as pottery and wall painting, a comparable working of

copper and a similar method of building tumuli and pyramids. The most striking example of this parallelism is found in the similarity (more apparent than intrinsic) of the Central American and Egyptian pyramids.

This apparent similarity of European and American cultures and the existence in America of legends about a land lost under circumstances similar to those mentioned by Plato in his account of Atlantis are held by some to be among the strongest arguments in favour of the existence of a 'lost island'. It is contended that before its destruction this island was a land bridge across the Atlantic; and that after its submersion the survivors sought refuge in the continents to east and west—on which they had already established themselves. This latter point, so the proponents of this theory say, can be argued from Plato's statement that the migration of the islanders of Atlantis to Europe preceded the disappearance of the island.

Against all this fantasy, it must be emphasized that, according to the accepted view, early man came to America from Asia during or after the last glacial period. The Red Indians are undoubtedly a Mongolian race deriving from eastern Asia. During the Ice Age, as previously stated, there was a land bridge linking Siberia and Alaska across what is now the Bering Strait. This was undoubtedly used and a cultural centre must have developed in the region of north-west America. When the ice sheets began diminishing about 11,000 years ago, a route was opened through the high plains east of the Rockies; and the break-up of the ice allowed a rapid migration of Arctic peoples southwards. When the ice sheets dwindled,

Supposed resemblances between the cultures on either side of the Atlantic have been advanced as evidence of the former existence of a common source in Atlantis. The examples illustrated here are from Ignatius Donnelly's *Atlantis: the Antediluvian World*. The pyramids of Egypt (*top left*) are compared with those of Mexico (*top right*). The vaulted arch above the entrance of the Treasury of Atreus at Mycenae, in Greece (*left*), is compared with a vaulted arch at Las Monjas in Central America (*far left*).

71

the sea level rose and the Arctic Ocean was covered with ice; and so as the Arctic populations migrated southwards, the door was closed for further migration from Siberia; as the sea-level rose, the Bering Strait came into existence and Siberia was again cut off from Alaska. And at the same time the continuous retreat of the ice sheets allowed the spread of the people from the Arctic regions of America down into South America in the course of a few thousand years.

The linguistic and anthropological similarities between the inhabitants of the Old and New Worlds—such as they are—and all the ethnographical data can be readily explained on these lines without invoking the existence of any large island lying across the Atlantic.

10. The argument from legends of the Flood

The existence in America of legends involving the disappearance of a piece of land under conditions comparable with Plato's account of the end of Atlantis is brought forward in arguments allied with the previous discussion; and it raises several interesting points.

First, one must take into consideration the fact that all the peoples of the world suffer at some time from much the same natural phenomena. Earthquakes, destructive sea-waves or *tsunamis* (as the Japanese call them), volcanic eruptions and floods occur in almost every part of the earth. These phenomena are more frequent and particularly violent in all the regions round the Pacific basin and in the Caribbean. Since these manifestations are generated by the same natural processes, the disasters they cause are very similar and human reactions to them more or less the same all over the world. Human reactions being similar, human progress tends to follow the same lines in material, intellectual and spiritual developments; and the independent existence of similar but unrelated traditions in various parts of the world is readily conceivable.

That there is in Guatemala a myth of a world catastrophe similar to the Greek myth of Phaethon (who was allowed to drive the chariot of his father, the sun, with disastrous consequences) is not surprising. The flashing arcs observed in the sky during violent volcanic eruptions combined with the falling of ash may account for the myth of Phaethon, son of Helios, and the burning up of all that was on earth (*Tim.*, *22C*), and also for the legends similar to it. It is interesting, in view of what will appear later, that the conflagration of Phaethon was considered contemporary with the Greek legend of the Flood, in which Deucalion and Pyrrha were the sole survivors.

This story of Deucalion's Flood bears a striking resemblance to the biblical tradition of Noah's Flood and the Babylonian myth of the flood. In all these myths the flood is a punishment from the gods. The chosen one of the gods is forewarned about the impending catastrophe and takes all the necessary steps to save the members of his family and various animals and plants. These myths, and the Mexican and Guatemalan

Lightning displays and falls of ash during volcanic eruptions may be the origin of the myth of Phaethon. (Photograph taken during the eruption of Surtsey in 1963.)

73

myths of a deluge together with the existence of similar traditions, have given rise to the belief that all the floods mentioned in them were the same flood which occurred simultaneously throughout the world. This cannot be accepted: local disasters of this kind can be sudden and cataclysmic, world-scale floods are so slow as to pass almost unnoticed during one human generation.

According to H. E. Suess, between 90,000 and 11,000 years ago the temperature began to fall at the rate of one degree Centigrade every 11,000 years. But about 11,000 years ago the temperature began to rise abruptly—i.e. at the rate of one degree Centigrade every 1,000 years. This increase continued until a few thousand years ago; and for the last few thousand years, temperatures have remained at about as high as the maximum value which was reached during all the Pleistocene inter-glacial stages. The 'abrupt' increase in temperature—one degree Centigrade per 1,000 years—which caused the waning of the ice sheets, most certainly passed unnoticed by the peoples of that time.

Many of those who have advanced theories on the problem of Atlantis have lacked geological knowledge and have failed to realize the geological context of this word 'abrupt'; and they have attributed the waning of the ice sheets (supposedly brought about by the *abrupt* increase in temperature) to the sudden disappearance of the territory of Atlantis. The geological time-scale was assumed by them to be a human time-scale of events occurring in the short period of one human generation.

The view that the submersion and disappearance of Atlantis must have caused a lowering of sea level or a retreat of the sea and that such a change manifested itself in the Mediterranean is geologically without foundation. It has been proved that since the last glacial retreat, about 11,000 years ago, the sea level has risen, not fallen. In Europe the eustatic movement of sea level, caused by the melting of large masses of inland ice, began during the Seventh or Eighth Millennium BC. The upward movement was not continuous but alternated with periods of stability and even fall in sea level. Since the first century BC the sea level must have risen 8–9 ft (2·5–2·8).

On the rocky coasts of the Aegean island of Siphnos there are holes made by lithophagous (or stone-boring) molluscs at 2,300 ft (700 m) above the present sea level; and similar phenomena in other parts of Greece and elsewhere in Europe are recorded by Ph. Negris. These are not due to eustatic changes in sea level of the order of several hundred metres but to the slow, upward continental or epeirogenic movement of the land since the Pliocene Age, i.e., at least 1,000,000 years before the last glacial period. In the opinion of M. C. Dollfus the sea level has not conspicuously changed since the Pliocene. The generally accepted view is that in recent times only the continents rise continuously or subside locally and un-evenly. The change in sea level caused by eustatic movement does not exceed 55 fathoms (100 m).

The upward and downward movement of the land during such

epeirogenic periods and the rate involved in such changes may be illust-rated by the isostatic movements observed in the old terrestrial shields of the Baltic and of Canada. Isostatic movement, roughly speaking, is that adjustment which takes place with an alteration of gravity or trans-ference of weight. An example is the uplift of the land in Finland and Scandinavia caused by the continuous melting of the inland ice which had covered them during the last Ice Age. Now the rate of this particular uplift is one metre per century at most. As can be easily understood, this can have no short-term effect on man; the inhabitants of Scandinavia have no personal consciousness of the phenomenon and their only know-ledge of it derives from geological studies.

As will have appeared in this lengthy chapter, there have been very many proponents of the theory that Atlantis lay in the Atlantic Ocean; and many and curious have been the arguments put forward in support of this theory. It has seemed right to examine all of these and to show their weakness. At this point it is perhaps necessary to summarize a few con-clusions.

There never was an Atlantic land bridge since the arrival of man in the world; there is no sunken land mass in the Atlantic; the Atlantic Ocean must have existed in its present form for at least a million years. In fact it is a geophysical impossibility for an Atlantis of Plato's dimensions to have existed in the Atlantic.

Are there any other locations put forward? There are indeed.

FIVE
Other Sites

The Atlantic Ocean has no monopoly as the suggested site of Atlantis; other oceans and continents have been suggested, one after the other, as the cradle of earth's first civilization. In fact there are few places in the world, where traces of prehistoric culture have been discovered, which have not been considered as either the homeland or a colony of the Atlanteans. Writers have seriously supported the claims of Palestine, Sweden, the region between Ireland and Brittany, the Heligoland regions of the North Sea, the Arctic, Central Asia, Nigeria, Tunisia and Spain. All the theories supporting the places as the location of Atlantis have the same serious disadvantage: they lack any geological evidence that in any of them was there ever any sudden sinking of the land sufficiently great to cause serious destruction.

1. Tunisia

In the opinion of A. Herrmann (1930) the plain that Plato mentions is a small one in Shott-el-Jerid, in Tunisia between Nefta and the bay of Gabes. As Herrmann himself admits, this region did not sink; on the contrary it rose, the sea moved away from it, and it was finally covered by the sands of the Sahara. Incidentally, the Shott-el-Jerid region is the most earthquake-free district in all North Africa.

2. Tartessos

Equally earthquake-free is the south-west coast of Spain; but if one were to accept the views of H. Schulten (1922) the metropolis of Atlantis was the famous town of Tartessos, at the mouth of the Guadalquivir, north of Cadiz. The lack of any geological evidence that Tartessos was destroyed by an earth catastrophe led Schulten to suggest that after the destruction of the town by the Carthaginians and their closing of the Straits of Gibraltar in 509 BC Greek seamen lost trace of the town. The 'disappearance' of the town in this manner is, according to Schulten, the event that gave rise to the myth of the submersion of Atlantis. Unfortunately for this theory, however, the Atlantis story was brought from Egypt by Solon (639–558 BC) many decades before the destruction of Tartessos and the closing of the Straits. Furthermore, this theory leaves many points in

The shallow water round north-west France and the British Isles has suggested to some writers that Atlantis was submerged in this region. In fact, what was dry land here was submerged by a very slow, regular rise in sea level at the end of the last Ice Age, not by movement of the land. The shaded area shows the 100-metre isobath.

Overleaf Although the Atlantic Ocean is the most favoured location of Atlantis, scores of others have been proposed by theorists of every kind. Deserts are seen as former oceans, islands as submerged mountain peaks, and the remains of ancient cultures as the remnants of lost Atlantis.

Plato's story unexplained, notably the annihilation of the Athenian army during the submersion of the island.

3. North-west France

F. Gidon has argued that the Atlantis legend is a conglomeration of many traditions from various sources; and that the story of the submersion refers, in his view, to the flooding of the coasts of north-western France. The region inundated is now defined by the 100 m isobath (i.e. line of equal depth). The extent of this region in a north-westerly direction is almost equal to the present breadth of France. Relying on botanical criteria, Gidon claims that the region which formerly joined Brittany with Ireland was inundated during the Bronze Age (somewhere between, say, 3000 and 1200 BC). The metropolis of Atlantis had, he thinks, been built on a coastal terrace formed by an uplift in Neolithic times, while the three zones of waters and two zones of land surrounding the metropolis consisted of a network of artificial rivers and dunes. The inundation of the region stretching between Brittany and Ireland, as well as the formation of the English Channel and the North Sea, is ascribed by him to a slow

YUCATAN
BAHAMAS
ANTILLES
NEWFOUNDLAND
GREENLAND
ICELAND
COLOMBIA
VENEZUELA
PERU
ATLANTIC
OCEAN
English Cha
NW
Azores
Portugal
Basque
Provinces
Madeira
Tartessos
Spain
Gibraltar
Canary Islands
Morocco
Atlas Mountains
BOLIVIA
Cape Verde Islands
ALGERIA
BRAZIL
SAHAR
NIGERIA
PATAGONIA
St Helena

sinking of the land which began during the Neolithic period and continued until AD 800.

However, geological data show that the inundation of the north-west coast of France and the formation of the English Channel were caused by an overflow of the sea during the Holocene period following the end of the Ice Age. This overflow, which is known as the Flanders Transgression, began about 7000 BC. Its maximum was reached in 5400 BC; but in 2400 BC the level of the sea dropped by about 2 metres, although about 400 years later a renewed rise in sea-level with consequent flooding was observed—as proved by Sir Gavin de Beer from the submersion of the Mount's Bay forest opposite Penzance, in Cornwall.

This Flanders Transgression was caused either by a sinking of the land or by eustatic movements of sea level, or both. The sea-level rise from eustatic movement cannot have exceeded 55 fathoms (100 m); such rises are very slow and the results not noticeable in the course of a single human generation. According to Wolff, Heligoland and the Elbe estuary on the German coast of the North Sea have subsided only $6\frac{1}{2}$ ft (2 m) in 4,000 years at an average rate, therefore, of 2 in. (5 cm) per 100 years. According to Stille, the greatest vertical movements ever observed do not exceed 5 metres per 100 years. In addition the English Channel and North Sea areas have never suffered from serious earthquakes.

Plato states specifically that the land zones encircling the metropolis of Atlantis were rocky. This means that they could not have been dunes, which are sand formations. In addition Atlantis had very high mountains which could not have been covered by water which is only 110 fathoms (200 m) deep. And, finally, all the low-lying coasts of the world were flooded with water during the eustatic rise of sea level following the last Ice Age, and so all continental shelves defined by the 55 fathom (100 m) line could on this argument be advanced as submerged sections of Atlantis.

PLATE 5. The cliffs of the Santorin caldera, below Oea, recalling Plato's description of the red, black and white rocks used for building in Atlantis.

4. Heligoland

This entertaining theory was advanced in 1953 by Jürgen Spanuth, a pastor of Bordelum in Germany. He claims that the Metropolis of Atlantis was exactly 50 stades (about 5·7 miles) north-east of Heligoland, where remains of an abruptly destroyed settlement have been found in $4\frac{1}{2}$ fathoms (8 m) of water in the higher part of a submarine ridge, known as Steingrund. Spanuth believes that the Atlantis story, as brought to Greece by Solon, is a description of the calamities which destroyed the Minoan, Mycenaean and Hittite civilizations and devastated Egypt in about 1220 BC, i.e. a few decades before the Pharaoh Rameses III (1200–1168 BC) mounted the throne. He stresses the fact that there is considerable agreement between Plato's story of Atlantis and the description of the disasters recorded in the reliefs on the Medinet Habu columns. In the temple of Amun, in ancient Egyptian Thebes (now known as Medinet Habu), there

Overleaf PLATE 6. Another view of the coloured rocks of the caldera walls, south of Phera.

Overleaf, facing page PLATE 7. The Santorin lagoon, from the town of Phera. In the foreground a zigzag path winds down to the quay, and in the distance is the island of Therasia. Part of Nea Kameni is visible in the middle distance.

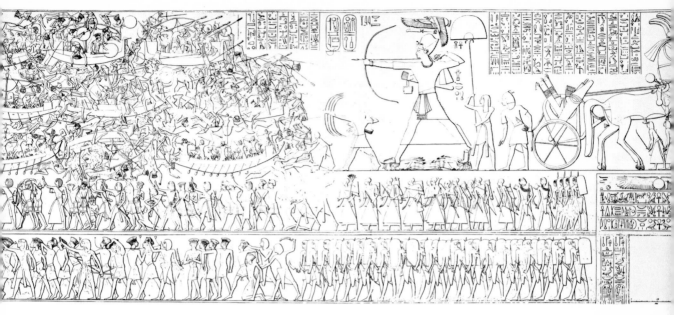

The victory of Rameses III over the 'Sea Peoples', commemorated in his temple at Medinet Habu. Some writers on Atlantis believe that the feathered headdresses and round shields indicate that the Sea Peoples came from the North Sea and were survivors of the Atlantis disaster.

are representations of the sea battle between Rameses III and the 'Sea Peoples', at the mouth of the Nile. Arguing from the shape of the ships, the round shields, the feathered headdress and other features of Rameses' opponents the German pastor then concludes that the peoples who made the sea raid on Egypt were from the North Sea—particularly from the area between Heligoland and Schleswig-Holstein. As for the destruction of the Royal Island of Atlantis, he claims that this was swallowed up by sea waves set up by the contemporaneous eruption not only of Santorin, but also of Etna, Hekla and other volcanoes, some in Sinai and others in other parts of the world—and by the falling of the comet called Phaethon in the mouth of the river Eider in the North Sea, near the North Friesian Islands. The authors' struggles to reconcile all these data hardly call for comment, but, in the light of what will appear later, it should be mentioned that they deny the accuracy of the dating (by archaeological and radiocarbon methods) of the Santorin eruption.

In listing the metals used by the inhabitants of Atlantis Plato mentions 'orichalcum'. According to Spanuth, this means 'amber'. Now amber is not a metal but a fossil resin, and was widely used as an ornament in Greece from at least 1500 BC. It was also much used in Plato's time and known by its proper name of 'electron'.

In the *Critias*, Plato says 'The ten princes . . . hunted after the bulls with staves and nooses but with *no weapons of iron*'. This could be taken to mean that they had iron weapons but did not use them in this case; but it is highly questionable. It is moreover the only reference to iron in the Atlantis story; and in any case the presumed possible use of iron is not sufficient to date the destruction of Atlantis to the beginning of the Iron Age, even supposing the time limits of the Bronze and Iron Ages were hard and fast or everywhere the same.

PLATE 8. The Kameni islands at sunset, photographed from the roof of the Hotel Atlantis in Phera.

As regards the round shields and the feathered headdress, Spanuth ignores the fact that these also appear in the hieroglyphs of the famous clay 'Phaistos disc'. Whatever may be the origins of this disc (and its significance), it was found in the Palace of Phaistos in Crete in a room containing Middle Minoan IIIB vases and a tablet in Linear A script, and is therefore admitted to be of the seventeenth or sixteenth century BC— i.e. at least 400 years before the sea-raid on Egypt.

In restating his case in 1965 Jürgen Spanuth says the sea-raid on Egypt was made by North Sea peoples who survived the swallowing up by the sea of the Royal Island of Atlantis. This is in direct contradiction with the order of events in Plato's story. Here in the *Timaeus* (*25C* and *D*) it is stated that the people of Atlantis attempted 'by one single onslaught' to enslave Egypt and Attica, but were defeated by the Athenians. 'But *at a later time* there occurred portentous earthquakes and floods' which swallowed up alike the Athenian army and the island of Atlantis.

Spanuth and his follower, Dr Günther Kehnscherper, have compiled

Feathered headdresses and round signs that may indicate shields are among the hiero-glyphs on the Phaistos disc, which was found at Phaistos in southern Crete. The disc dates from a period at least four hundred years before the sea raid repelled by Rameses III.

quantities of relevant (and irrelevant) data but ignore the point so well stated by Professor Rhys Carpenter, that 'the occurrence of archaeological material with Late Minoan connections beneath the volcanic debris on Santorin, coupled with the entire absence of any reported traces from the heyday of Mycenaean prosperity anywhere on the island, combines to exculpate Santorin from having contributed to the decline of the Mycenaean civilization, since this decline belongs to a period at least a couple of centuries after the great eruption'.

Among other important points that these learned amateurs overlook are the facts that volcanic bombs could not possibly have been thrown a distance of 1,250 miles (2,000 km) or even a tenth of it; and that the Heligoland region of the North Sea was not formed 'in a single day and night'. The island of Heligoland now has a periphery of less than 5 km; but, arguing from historic rates of coastal recession, this was about 70 km in AD 1300 and about 200 km in AD 800. The geological evidence leaves no doubt that the German Bay, in which Heligoland stands, has been formed as a result of coastal recession, subsidences and eustatic movement of sea-level over many thousands of years. Moreover, as previously stated, the North Sea area is stable and immune from earthquakes.

5. Planetary collisions and Gondwanaland

Other theories about the location of Atlantis either ignore the geological event of the submersion or explain it by calling up bizarre and completely imaginary extraterrestrial phenomena which are directly contradicted by geological and cosmological science relating to the history of the earth and solar system. Velikovsky, for example, relies on the mythological traditions of certain peoples and claims that Venus originated as a comet in the Second Millennium BC. In the middle of that millennium it twice made contact with the earth and changed its cometary orbit; and in fact was still a comet during the tenth to eighth centuries BC. Colonel A. Braghine believes that the destruction of Atlantis was the result of a collision between the earth and a planet which was captured by the earth's gravity-field and became its satellite. With the passage of time the orbit of this satellite became smaller and smaller (owing to the earth's gravitational pull) and finally the satellite entered the earth's atmosphere and collided with the earth. In this collision Atlantis was submerged and a large continent, situated in the Indian Ocean, perished. Madagascar, Southern India, the Indian Ocean archipelagoes, Sumatra and some Pacific archipelagoes could be presumed to be among the surviving remnants of this lost continent, which was given the name of Lemuria and, later, Gondwana. In Braghine's view, Gondwana was inhabited by human beings before the appearance of the Moon, and in this context he regards Gondwana as the birthplace of man. In order to reconcile the myths of various people he supposes that the Earth had formerly two

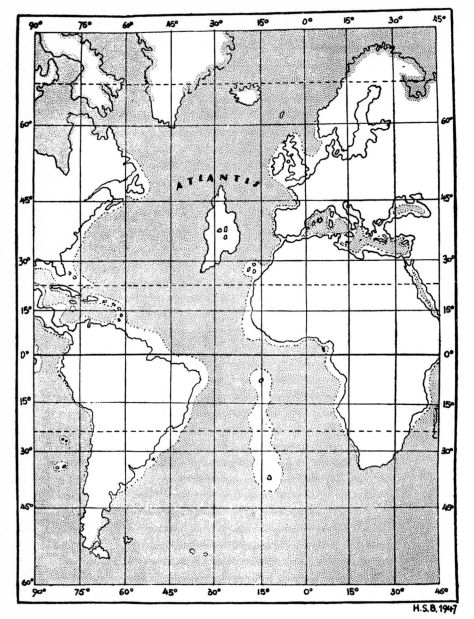

H.S.B. 1947

**Tentative map of the Outer Sea before the capture of Luna,
showing the approximate position of Atlantis**

Some writers have maintained that the moon was originally a wandering planet whose capture caused the Atlantis cataclysm: map from *The Atlantis Myth*, by H. S. Bellamy, published in 1948.

satellites, the Moon likewise being a planet captured by the earth's gravitational field and, according to him, also fated eventually to collide with the earth.

This flight of fancy, which does not even deserve the name of theory, is based on certain Greek mythological stories about *Proselenes* (or pre-Moon men) and similar legends of other peoples, chiefly Arabs and Hindus; and it is in complete contradiction with everything that is known about the Solar System and the structure and composition of the floor of the Indian Ocean and the date of its origin.

First, the structure and shape of the Indian Ocean do not justify any view of its having originated from the collision of the earth with an extra-terrestrial body. The shape of its basin in no way resembles the crater-like scar which would have been left by such an unlikely event in recent geological time. In addition to the reasons given in the preceding chapter for believing that ocean basins have never been continents, there is direct evidence from the composition of the floor of the Indian Ocean that it is similar to other oceans of the world and has never been a continent. The basalt in the floor of the Indian Ocean differs chemically from the basalt of the plateau magmas of the continents of the world in having a lower total iron content. The Indian Ocean, like the Atlantic and the Pacific, does not possess the sialic layer which is the characteristic continental layer; and the thickness of the earth's crust under it is not much more than 12 miles (20 km). And, again, geological evidence shows that the great basin of the Indian Ocean (which is more than 2,200 fathoms (4,000 m) deep) and particularly its western sector, took its present shape between the end of the Mesozoic and the beginning of the Tertiary, i.e. long before man appeared on the Earth.

As for the alleged former great continent of Gondwana, J. D. H. Wiseman has shown that rock fragments from the Carlsberg Ridge—which represents a major feature of the Indian Ocean floor—are definitely of submarine origin and chemically quite different from the basalts extruded into the beds of the sub-continent of India towards the end of the Cretaceous or possibly in Lower Eocene times. From this chemical dissimilarity and the fact that the radium content of the plateau basalts of the Indian Peninsula is very much greater than that of the Carlsberg Ridge basalts, Wiseman was led to believe that the theory held by Suess and his followers that a large area of Gondwana now lies submerged to the west of India is highly improbable.

Incidentally, the original pretext on which the former existence of a continent of Gondwana was imagined, namely the geographical distribution of certain fossil plants in the Palaeozoic Era (the *Glossopteris* flora), is now dropped, because these plants are not restricted to the Southern Hemisphere but have been found in Europe. As for the alleged similarity between the lemurs of Madagascar and of Asia—to explain which the former existence of a continent of Lemuria extending across the Indian Ocean was required—S. Millot has conclusively shown that such a similarity does not exist.

As regards the legends of 'pre-Moon men' and the like, we are left with an absurd dilemma: either these traditions, whether Greek, Hindu or Arab, derive not only from a time before the existence of *Homo sapiens*, or the submersion of Gondwana took place at a date so late as to be geologically impossible.

To summarize: conclusions relating to astronomical, anthropological and geological aspects and based on mythology, folklore, place-names and linguistics have increased the bibliography of Atlantis enormously without offering the slightest help in the solution of the riddle of the disappearance of Atlantis. The disappearance of an island is a geological event; and any attempt to explain this event on a basis of comparative philology, archaeology, anthropology, ethnography and the history of civilization must also be in accordance with geography—both historical and prehistorical—geology in general, and palaeontology. Science is one and indivisible, and conclusions reached in any one branch cannot be considered sound if they do not agree with observations and evidence in other branches or at least in those closely connected. This principle, fundamental to any serious research, has been ignored by amateur investigators and those one can call followers of the apocryphal arts. The most astounding explanations of the Atlantis submersion have been put forward: the absurdity of many of them led Franz Susemihl, a nineteenth-century translator of, and commentator on, Plato, to remark that if all the theories on Atlantis could be collected one would obtain a very good historical contribution to our knowledge of human insanity.

The solution, then, of the Atlantis enigma must be scientific, logical and consistent. Is such a solution possible?

Section 3

GEOPHYSICAL THEORIES AND FACTS

SIX
Geophysical and Archaeological Aspects

All the theories on the location of Atlantis which we have discussed so far ignore the factor of geological time, and the fact that the subsidence of a large island in a day and night is geologically impossible. The submersion of a large island or land-mass can and does happen—but over a period of centuries, and at such a slow rate as to be imperceptible in a single human generation; and these humanly imperceptible subsidences bring about no sensational destruction or catastrophe.

It is quite firmly established that the average of displacement of the earth's crust does not exceed something like 1 metre per 100 years. Between 1885 and 1950 the rise of sea-level all over the world was between 1·3 and 1·5 millimetres a year. Even when the ice sheets were melting faster, this rate did not exceed 5 mm a year. The yearly subsidence of the Atlantic coasts of the United States between 1930 and 1948 was 5·7 mm. In the Baltic Sea the uplift of the land owing to the melting of the ice-cap is now 11·3 mm a year. 15,000 years ago, when the ice was melting much faster, the uplift was 30 mm a year and by 12,000 years ago the rate had declined to 15 mm a year. During the next 500 years, it is estimated the yearly uplift in this area will not exceed 5 mm. In the Cherbourg region, on the north coast of France, the annual uplift between 1885 and 1950 was 1·8 mm. Even in Java—one of the world's most active regions, as regards both earthquakes and volcanoes—the uplift does not exceed 10 mm a year.

In total and in the course of very long periods of time such movements as these can effect considerable changes; but obviously their effect 'in a day and night' is hardly perceptible. The disappearance of a land-mass in a (humanly) short space of time is geologically possible under two conditions alone:

(1) After severe earthquakes, when the banks of lakes or rivers or sea coasts break off, as happened, for example, in the winter of 373 BC when Helice, on the south coast of the Gulf of Corinth, slipped into the sea.

(2) In the case of volcanic paroxysm, owing to the emptying of the magma chamber and the collapse of the roof of the cavity thus produced, as happened around 1500 BC, when the central part of Santorin collapsed.

The breaking away of banks and sea coasts is sometimes of considerable extent. In mid-September 1716, a piece of land, 9·7 sq. miles in area (25 sq. km) slumped into the Yangtse-Kiang river near Nanking. During the Aegean earthquake of 26 December 1861, a piece of land 5 sq. miles

This nineteenth-century engraving (*left*) embodies the popular conception of the catastrophic effects of earthquakes; in fact, even the most severe earthquakes only occasionally cause fissures in the ground large enough to swallow human beings. The photograph (*right*) was taken at Valdivia in Chile during the great earthquake of 1960.

(13 sq. km) in area between the rivers Meganites and Erasinos—near where the town of Helice disappeared in 373 BC—slid under the sea. Such submersions are usually due to landslides of unconsolidated material on steep slopes or to the collapse of rocks which have been undercut.

The displacements produced by the sudden uplift or subsidence of land-masses during severe earthquakes rarely exceed 23 ft (7 m). The greatest vertical displacement which has been observed is $52\frac{1}{2}$ ft (16 m)—during the Alaska earthquake of 1899.

Cracks and fissures associated with violent earthquakes—despite popular belief—are seldom large enough to 'engulf' animals or people. In the records of earthquakes, the only authenticated cases are of a cow which was crushed in a fissure during the San Francisco earthquake of April 1906; and of a woman, during the Japanese earthquake of 28 June 1948. Another woman was reported to have been swallowed by the earth during the Ecuador earthquake on 5 August 1949.

The sensational effects are usually those associated with the sliding or collapse of unconsolidated material or loose earth on steep slopes. During an earthquake in New Guinea, for example, on 15 September 1906, a

landslide buried about 100 natives. On the Malayan island of Great Sange on 14 March 1931 an earthquake-induced landslide buried the village of Lesabe and its 200 inhabitants. During the great Japanese earthquake of 1 September 1923 loose material amounting to over 1,000,000 cubic metres traversed a valley 160 yards wide and 3·75 miles (6 km) long with an average gradient of six degrees in the space of 5 minutes. It covered the village of Nebukava and its 700 inhabitants, destroyed the railway station and carried away a passenger train with all its crew and passengers. On 23 June 1925 a landslide of 50,000,000 cu. yards completely blocked the Gros Ventre river in Wyoming, U.S.A.; and in Montana on 7 August 1959 a similar landslide with a content estimated at 34–43 million cu. yards blocked the Madison river, six miles south of the Hebgen dam. In this last case a new lake came into being and 26 persons were buried alive.

Major earthquakes may have very large death-rolls. The Messina earthquake of 1908 killed 103,000 persons. During the great Tokyo earthquake of 1923, the dead, injured and those lost in the great sea wave exceeded 246,000. The most destructive earthquake in the seismological record is that which took place in China on 23 January 1556. According to Kuo Tseng-Chien, the casualties were over 800,000. Such losses, of course, occur in densely populated areas, for as a rule the destructive

effects of earthquakes are comparatively restricted in area. During the great Lisbon earthquake of 1 November 1755, the greatest recorded at the time, the average radius of the damaged area did not exceed 375 miles (600 km), although the earthquake shock was felt at distances of up to 1,250 miles (2,000 km). From the area which felt the shock it may be concluded that its magnitude was between $8\frac{3}{4}$ and 9 on the Richter instrumental scale. No severer earthquake has been observed.

That these are all relatively modern examples does not affect the argument. Rocks possess a certain yield-strength, and strain cannot be built up over a certain value. The elasticity of rocks increases with their age and the strain a layer of rock can stand without breaking is greater than that which the same layer could withstand when it was younger. The mountain-building forces may have been greater in the past, but the strain they built up in a given mass of rocks must have been less than, or at most equal to, the amount which can now be built up in the same conditions. Therefore it follows that the frequency of earthquakes may have been greater in the past, but not their magnitude. Earthquake magnitude, or the area over which it is felt, depends on the amount of energy released during the faulting of the rock layers; but the amount of seismic energy cannot exceed the amount of elastic energy accumulated before faulting.

In view of all this and bearing in mind what Plato wrote, it is clear that a geological event in the Atlantic, or even in the Western Mediterranean, could not possibly have caused the destruction of the whole Athenian army.

In this spectacular nineteenth-century engraving of the famous Lisbon earthquake of 1755, the collapse of buildings and the subsequent destruction caused by fires and seismic sea waves are shown occurring simultaneously, instead of in sequence.

Such an occurrence could have happened only if the whole Athenian army was on an island that sank—an eventuality that is not probable. The island vanished *after* the war, but the Athenians were carrying on a war of liberation. Only a war of aggression could explain the presence of an Athenian army on the island of Atlantis. In addition, in the Atlantis story there is a clear distinction between the way the Athenian army perished and the way the island of Atlantis disappeared.

According to Plato the army was 'swallowed up by the earth' while the island was 'swallowed up by the sea'. This would seem clearly to indicate that the army was buried on land. As mentioned above, the faults or fissures associated with earthquakes are never large enough to 'swallow up' persons in quantity. Therefore the Athenian army must have been buried either under a thick layer of volcanic ash or under a large land-slide or earth-avalanche. The former structure of the ground on which the city of Athens was built and its destruction at the same time as Atlantis supports this view.

Let us recall exactly what Plato said (in the *Critias*, *112*):

'In the first place, the Acropolis, as it existed then, was different from what it is now. For as it is now, the action of a single night of extraordinary rain has crumbled it away and made it bare of soil, when earthquakes occurred simultaneously with the third of the disastrous floods which preceded the destructive deluge in the time of Deucalion. But in its former extent, it went down towards the Eridanus and the Ilissus, and embraced within it the Pnyx, and had the Lycabettus as its boundary over against the Pnyx; and it was all rich in soil and, save for a small space, level on the top. . . . And near the place of the present Acropolis there was one spring—which was choked up by the earthquake so that but small trick-lings of it are now left round about; but to the men of that time it afforded a plentiful stream for them all, being well tempered both for winter and summer.'

It is a well-known fact that Attica does not suffer from disastrous local earthquakes, but to cause a disturbance in the ground water of the Athens Acropolis the focus of the earthquake concerned must have been not far from Attica. The longest distances at which severe disturbances in the circulation of underground water have been observed do not exceed 125 miles (200 km) from the epicentre of the earthquake. Moreover it was previously shown that the longest distance from the epicentre at which very small damage may be observed does not exceed 375 miles (600 km). All the places, however, which have been previously discussed and suggested as possible locations for the 'lost island' are more than 625 miles (1,000 km) from Athens. All such distant locations therefore must be ruled out as possible sites for Atlantis. The only acceptable location is in the Eastern Mediterranean.

The first attempt to locate Atlantis in the Eastern Mediterranean was made by Bortolli in 1780. He formulated the view that the Atlantis story was invented by Solon and later used by Plato. Bortolli then maintained that in Plato's version the islanders of Atlantis are in fact the Persians, and that the Atlantis story is a version of the wars between the Athenians and the Persians transformed into a myth. With this reading Atlantis must be the theatre of the war and, so, Attica, of which Athens was the capital. Latreille (1879) also held that Atlantis should be sought in Attica.

In the latter part of the nineteenth century, French excavations aroused some interest in Santorin. At this stage it will be sufficient to say that Santorin or Santorini is the name given to three islands, Thera, Therasia and Aspronisi, which are the remains of a volcanic island lying about 78 miles north-north-east of Crete. The volcanologist Fouqué excavated on Therasia in 1866 and the archaeologists Gorceix and Mamet dug on Thera and Therasia in 1870. Their finds were of great interest and showed that the island, of which the present islands are the remains, had a very advanced culture before the submersion of its central part and the covering of the remainder with a thick layer of pumice. Among the finds were quantities of stone tools, decorated pottery and utensils made of lava, including millstones, basins and mortars. In many of the vessels remains of barley, peas, lentils and straw were found. Among the tools was a saw made of pure copper. The bones of sheep and goats were found: and in one of the houses uncovered near Akrotiri in south-east Thera there was a painted plaster wall.

From these finds the archaeologists concluded that the ancient inhabitants of Santorin used weights and measures and possessed a system of numeration. They produced lime to make plaster, built vaults and

Among the finds made on Santorin in the eighteen-sixties and subsequently were a copper saw (*left*), approximately nine inches long, and some decorated pottery (*right*).

made mural paintings. Agriculture flourished, and weaving and pottery had reached a high stage of accomplishment.

Relying on these conclusions, Louis Figuier expressed the opinion in 1872 that Plato's Atlantis was an island in the Aegean archipelago which had been submerged by a geological convulsion; and that this island could only be Santorin, part of which had evidently sunk into the sea while the remaining parts were covered with a thick layer of pumice. Under this layer, he suggested, towns and villages were buried in the same way that Pompeii and Herculaneum had been buried in the volcanic ash from the eruption of Vesuvius in AD 79.

On 19 January 1909 K. T. Frost, writing anonymously in *The Times*, advanced the theory that Plato's story of Atlantis was a garbled account of the destruction of Minoan Crete preserved in Egyptian records; and

a similar suggestion was made in 1917 by D. A. Mackenzie. At the same time excavations in Crete led the American geographer E. S. Balch to put forward the following theory before the American Geographical Society. According to Balch, Plato's story, while containing many anomalies difficult to resolve, suggested that Atlantis was an island which was the centre of a powerful state. This story, he believed, put one in mind of Crete and the Cretan empire of Minos. He maintained that the Cretan empire must have been destroyed around 1200 BC by the Athenians in alliance with the Egyptians, the legend of Theseus and the Minotaur being a mythical version of this war. The submersion of Atlantis is explained as an allegory of the end of the Cretan empire and its annihilation as a commercial and cultural centre; while the 'Pillars of Hercules' refer to passages between unspecified rocky islands of the Aegean. The location of Atlantis in the Mediterranean was supported by F. Butavandt, a little later, in 1925.

In 1947 Professor J. Koumaris submitted a paper to the Hellenic Anthropological Society in which he set forward the theory that the Atlantis story refers to a 'local catastrophe' produced by earthquakes or floods occurring in the Mediterranean. This same view had been put forward by the German naturalist Alexander von Humboldt about a century previously. According to Koumaris the occurrence was no doubt observed by the Egyptian priests and recorded by them with overstatements, particularly as regards the extent of the catastrophe. In consequence Plato 'gave an exaggerated written account of the exaggerations he had heard'—the story growing like a snowball rolling down a slope.

At the same session of the Hellenic Anthropological Society (24 November 1948) the distinguished Greek archaeologist, Professor Sp. Marinatos, supported the view that the Atlantis legend is a historical tradition which in characteristic manner developed into a conglomeration of historical events of various peoples. He said:

'The catastrophe of Thera, accompanied by tremendous natural phenomena and the simultaneous disappearance of the Cretans from Egypt gave rise to the myth of a submersion of a large and prosperous island. The invasions of the people from Italy (i.e. the 'Sea Peoples', who attacked Egypt on several occasions between 1300 BC and 1167, when they were defeated by Rameses III, and who included Achaeans, Danaans, Tyrrhenians, Sicilians and Sardinians) were added to the legend as invasions of 'Atlanteans'. Their successful repulse from Greece and the bravery of the Ionian mercenaries of the Saitic Pharaohs created the legend of a wonderful and invincible army of the Athenians. All these are facts that occurred successively within a period of 900 years (from 1500–600 BC) and were embodied in a single historical myth. The Egyptians had in the same manner ascribed to King Sesostris events that had occurred during whole centuries and thus created a myth. The Greeks did the same with Minos.'

PLATE 9. Two views of the stark landscape of Nea Kameni. In the distance are the cliffs of Thera south of the town of Phera, showing the horizontal strata of white *pozzolana* and dark lava which indicate that several successive eruptions must have occurred before the cataclysm that destroyed the centre of the island.

Overleaf PLATE 10. One of the volcanic craters on Nea Kameni. In the distance is part of the town of Merovigli.

Overleaf, facing page PLATE 11. The view from Nea Kameni to the cliffs of Thera, on which stands the town of Phera. The eroded brown lava in the foreground contrasts with the black lava of more recent eruptions.

Marinatos attributed the transference of Atlantis to the Atlantic Ocean to the fact that the Phoenicians had navigated the Atlantic in the reign of the Pharaoh Necho (609–593 BC). The marvellous stories which those daring seamen had certainly brought back to Egypt must have been current matter for discussion and would naturally form a basis on which to transfer Atlantis to the Atlantic Ocean.

This would indeed be a very probable and reasonable explanation of the 'transplanting' of the Atlantis story into the Atlantic Ocean. The reference to the 'Pillars of Hercules' (which are always taken to mean the Straits of Gibraltar) are, however, a difficulty and an anomaly in this explanation. Is it possible, then, that the 'Pillars of Hercules' are not the Straits of Gibraltar?

This has been the subject of some interesting conjectures. Nearly all the labours of Hercules were performed in the Peloponnese. The last and hardest of those which Eurystheus imposed on the hero was to descend to Hades and bring back its three-headed dog guardian, Cerberus. According to the most general version Hercules entered Hades through the abyss at Cape Taenarum (the modern Cape Matapan), the western cape of the Gulf of Laconia. The eastern cape of this gulf is Cape Maleas, a dangerous promontory, notorious for its rough seas.

Pausanias records that on either side of this windswept promontory were temples, that on the west dedicated to Poseidon, that on the east to Apollo. It is perhaps therefore not extravagant to suggest that the Pillars of Hercules referred to are the promontories of Taenarum and Maleas; and it is perhaps significant that the twin brother of Atlas was allotted the extremity of Atlantis closest to the Pillars of Hercules. The relevant passage in the *Critias* (*114A–B*) states:

'And the name of his younger twin-brother, who had for his portion the extremity of the island near the pillars of Heracles up to the part of the country now called Gadeira after the name of that region, was Eumelus in Greek, but in the native tongue Gadeirus—which fact may have given its title to the country.'

Since the region had been named after the second son of Poseidon, whose Greek name was Eumelus, its Greek title must likewise have been Eumelus, a name which brings to mind the most westerly of the Cyclades, Melos, which is in fact not far from the notorious Cape Maleas. The name Eumelus was in use in the Cyclades; and the ancient inscription ('Eumelus an excellent danger') was found on a rock on the island of Thera.

In general it can be argued from a number of points in Plato's narrative that placing 'the Pillars of Hercules' at the south of the Peloponnese makes sense, while identifying them with the Straits of Gibraltar does not. This way the scale and direction of the attack are correct, the Aegean archipelago provides a suitable geographical setting; while the religion of the Atlanteans, based on the worship of Poseidon, is obviously less and less likely the further removed it is from Greece and the Aegean scene.

PLATE 12. The temple of Apollo, part of the ruins of old Thira, a Greek and Hellenistic settlement on a col between Mount Prophet Elias and Cape Mesa Vouno, overlooking the sea on the south-east corner of Thera.

AEGEAN SEA

Northern Sporades

EUBOEA

Lesbos

Chios

Patras

Corinth

Athens
Mycenae
Aegina
Methana
Poros

ATTICA

Andros

Peloponnese

Mykonos
Delos
Paros

Seriphos

Siphnos
Antiparos
Naxos

Cyclades

Dodecanese

Patmos

Cos

Pylos

Antimolos

Melos

Nissyros

Gulf of
Laconia

Cape Maleas

Santorin

Anaphi

Cape Matapan

Christianon

Rhode

MEDITERRANEAN SEA

CRETE

Ionian Islands

SEVEN
Aegeis and Santorin

Since it begins to appear that the events of the Atlantis story—the submersion of Atlantis, the wiping out of an Athenian army, the drying up of the spring on the Acropolis of Athens—were accompanied by earthquakes and terrible floods and that these must have taken place within, say, 200 miles of Attica, it is necessary to look closely at the Aegean basin and to examine its geological history. Is the cataclysm necessary for such a series of disasters possible in this area? Is there any record of such a cataclysm?

In the middle of the Tertiary era, that is, about 30,000,000 years ago, the Greek peninsula, together with the Ionian Islands, Western Asia Minor and the Aegean Sea formed one block of land. This block, the results of the Alpine Folding which began in the Oligocene period and continued to the end of the Miocene, has been called 'Aegeis' by some geologists. Immediately after its formation, a series of faults and trench-like subsidences, such as the tectonic trench between Patras and Corinth, brought about a gradual breaking up of the Aegeis, accompanied by subsidences and upheavals of the fault-blocks. These epeirogenic movements of the rise and fall of the continent alternating with orogenic or mountain-building movements allowed the waters of the Mediterranean repeatedly to overflow the lower levels. As the result of the alternations, the Peloponnese twice became an island.

The penetration of the sea to the central part of Aegeis began mainly in the Quaternary era and continued until its end. As a result of the penetration—which lasted about 500,000 years—many valleys of that time were turned into the beautiful bays and harbours of today; and many mountain ranges into picturesque peninsulas and idyllic islands. Euboea, Crete, the Cyclades, the Dodecanese, Chios, Lesbos, the Northern and Thracian Sporades are the surviving parts of the land-mass which once joined Greece to Western Asia Minor. The fauna of Aegeis included pygmy elephants and bones of these animals have been found in Crete, Naxos, Seriphos and Delos.

The high volcanic and seismic activity and the great gravity anomalies which appear in the Aegean Sea, particularly in the south-eastern part, show that the alternating mountain-building movements that shaped it are still active in this region.

Volcanic activity began in the Aegean Sea region in the middle of the

The Aegean Sea, site of the Atlantis disaster.

Tertiary at the same time as the faulting and dislocation of the land-mass which previously joined Greece with Asia Minor. The extensive fragmentation of this land-mass allowed the volcanic magma to intrude into the cracks and fissures and to come up to the surface of Aegeis through the points of least resistance. In this way many volcanic centres were produced all over the Aegean Sea. Only three of these centres were still active during historic times, all three being in the Cycladic volcanic zone. This zone extends across the Aegean in the form of an arc with its convex side towards Crete. It includes the volcanic centres of Sousaki (near Calamaki), Aegina, Methana, Poros, Antimelos, Melos, Ananos, Kimolos, Polivos, Stronghylon, Despoticon, Antiparos, Santorin, Chistianon, Cos and Nissyros. Volcanic activity began in this zone in the Pliocene period, about 10,000,000 years ago. The Methana volcano has been extinct since 282 BC; the last eruption of the Nissyros volcano was in AD 1422; and the Santorin volcano was active in 1956.

Santorin today

Since we shall be concerned with Santorin—which is quite unlike any other Greek island, little-known even in Greece and rarely visited except by seismologists, volcanologists and, briefly, by passengers in cruise ships —it is worth while to give a picture of what the island is like today.

The only approach is by sea. The ship comes in through a gap between two islands (Thera and Therasia) and enters a huge circle of deep waters, 32 square miles in area, nearly 7 miles from north to south and $4\frac{2}{3}$ miles from east to west; its depth is between 300 and 400 metres, and no ship can anchor there. The circle of water is limited by the three islands of Santorin, the large crescent-shaped Thera on the east, north and south; the oblong Therasia on the west; and on the south-west between the other two the uninhabited islet of Aspronisi ('white island'). In the centre of the circle are two other islands, volcanic cones, the smaller Palaea Kameni and the larger Nea Kameni.

It immediately becomes apparent that the vast circle of waters is in fact the crater of a gigantic volcano and that the three islands which surround it are the shattered remains of the crater's walls. They rise almost sheer from the water at some points to 1,150 ft, at others somewhat less; they are fantastically banded in strata of greyish-white, faded black and a menacing dark red; and at the top of the rim, crowned with an almost embroidered border of dazzling white, are the houses and churches of the towns and villages of the two inhabited islands (plates 4, 5, 6, 7, 8).

Passengers land in small boats, at the quay at the bottom of a towering cliff; and on foot, or riding mules or donkeys, begin the zig-zag ascent to the summit. (No wheeled vehicle can tackle this climb of 500-odd steps between ramps and in seemingly endless hairpin bends.) They find themselves at last in Phera, an elongated township of brilliantly white-washed houses, shops, churches and cafés, intricately connected by narrow winding alleys filled with the traffic of mules and donkeys laden with goods

The Santorin group of islands, remnants of the Ancient Metropolis of Atlantis.

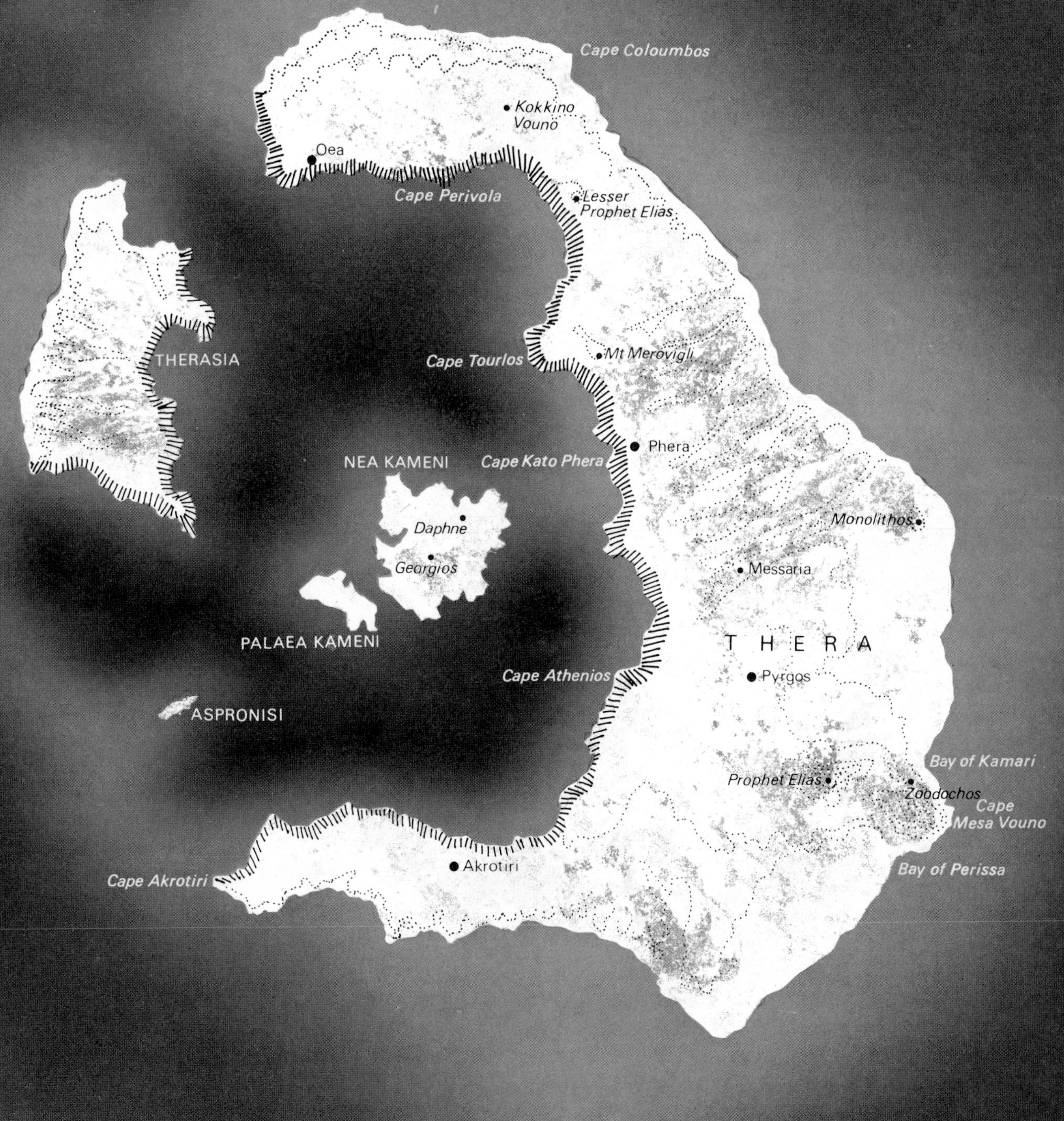

Cape Coloumbos

Kokkino
Vouno

Oea

Cape Perivola

Lesser
Prophet Elias

THERASIA

Cape Tourlos

Mt Merovigli

NEA KAMENI

Cape Kato Phera

Phera

Daphne

Monolithos

Georgios

Messaria

PALAEA KAMENI

T H E R A

ASPRONISI

Cape Athenios

Pyrgos

Bay of Kamari

Prophet Elias

Zoodochos
Cape
Mesa Vouno

Cape Akrotiri

Akrotiri

Bay of Perissa

from the harbour and produce from the countryside. For although the seaward view looks from the vertiginous cliffs over the deep blue waters of the crater, the landward view, though less spectacular, is equally fascinating. You are in effect looking down the sloping side of a mountain —which you have climbed from the interior—the talus of the original volcanic cone, which leads down to the sea. Two mountainous peaks limit this long curved slope, one at the southern extremity, called, not surprisingly, the Prophet Elias, crowned with a monastery and a NATO radar station; the other, at the northern end, called the Lesser Prophet Elias. In the middle of the vast panorama, on the edge of the sea, rises a citadel-like rock, Monolithos ('single stone'). But the totality of the landscape, diversified with occasional white villages and traversed by a few roads sometimes lined with gum trees, is made up of stone-walled green fields. It is an astonishing sight in this context. Are these mountain pastures? Are these really fields, green even in high summer? Impossible, for the island has little rainfall, few springs and imports its drinking water from Poros. The green fields are vineyards, expanses of grey volcanic dust supporting—heaven knows how—thousands upon thousands of almost prostrate grapevines, so tenacious of life that broken branches trodden into the dusty roads by passing donkeys take root and begin once more their seemingly endless life-span.

The fields of Thera, with Monolithos on the eastern shore of the island. In the distance is the island of Anaphi (foreshortened by telephoto lens).

103

Norman Douglas visited the island in 1892 and wrote (in *Looking Back*):
'Santorin was to be visited. Ever since reading Voswinkel's *De Theraeorum Insulis*—an incredibly dull inaugural dissertation, but useful because it gives the classical references—I had made up my mind on this point and collected all possible scraps of information about the island; and there are a good many of them. I found it a fantastic spot. Picturesque, or romantic, is too mild a term; the cliff scenery and the colours of sea and land made one catch one's breath. Under a bleak northern sky it would be a horrific kind of place; drenched in the glittering light of May it was fabulously beautiful. Whether I should be so susceptible nowadays is another question; the senses grow dulled, one sees so much! But Santorin is surely a vision which can disappoint nobody.'

True; and that visitor may be fortunate enough to see a Santorinian phenomenon which would have delighted Norman Douglas, gratifying both his pleasure in agricultural fertility and his strong mythmaking faculty. At dawn the sun rises beside the island of Anaphi and soon floods the eastern slopes of Thera in golden light. But it is not until late in the morning that its rays reach the waters of the crater, as these are shadowed by the tall cliffs. And these waters, being so deep, are colder than the surrounding sea, and when at last the sun does strike them in almost noonday heat, it draws up great clouds of water vapour, which, obedient to the laws of thermodynamics, rise in wraiths and swathes of mist up the cliffs in ever-changing pearly shapes—the delight of romantic painters, the origin of every nereid myth—which flood into the town and, still obedient to those rigid rules of thermodynamics, pour eastwards down the slopes and settle as an impalpable dew on the innumerable leaves of the myriad grapevines in a humidity which makes growth possible in a waterless land.

Volcanic dust is fertile and rich, granted the blessing of water even in small quantities, and Santorin exports wine, tomatoes, barley and beans; and the *pozzolana*, the great white strata of pumice and volcanic ash, which are the latest of the many layers of which the islands are made up, are mined for high-quality cement. Santorin is indeed a going concern. Yet bearing in mind the long history of eruption and earthquake, it must seem to the thoughtful visitor that man's tenure of this land is dangerous, precarious—almost miraculous. But, like the vine-branch trodden into the road by the donkey, it is also incredibly tenacious. On the surface and far below it are the evidences of man's occupation through thousands of years. Most notable are the remains of old Thira (plate 12), excavated at the end of the last century by the German, Hiller von Goertringen. These lie in the south-east of Thera on a col between the Prophet Elias and the peak of the cape called Mesa Vouno. It is a hair-raising site, caught by the winds which whistle between these two peaks and falling away in sheer precipices to the little bay of Perissa on the one side, and the bay of Kamari on the other. How could anyone choose to live here except in terror of attack? Yet for hundreds of years men did so choose—from the

In the caldera walls south of Phera, the *pozzolana* strata are mined for cement.

Geometric times of about 1000 BC through Greek, Ptolemaic and Roman
times well into the Byzantine age. Here in fact was a town over half a
mile long with temples, palaces, a colonnaded basilica and forum,
gymnasia and even a Greek theatre, its proscenium set against a sheer
drop to the levels of Kamari, 1,000 feet or so below—a wildly picturesque
competitor to whatever drama was being enacted before the formal
arches of the proscenium and on the semicircular orchestra.

But these are, after all, ruins; and the physical changes of man's history
in the island since then—Byzantine, Frankish, Venetian, Turkish—
although they do exist, notably as churches and Venetian fortifications,
are not conspicuous and are often ruinous. This is one of the great earthquake centres of the unquiet Aegean; man exists here, however tena-
ciously, on a precarious lease, liable to be terminated by the unpredictable
whims of vast natural forces. Nowhere is this more apparent than on the
major volcanic cone, the island of Nea Kameni.

The visitor reaches this in a boat from the little harbour of Phera and
lands in a secluded cove—a re-entrant between two, perhaps three,
different flows of lava. The head of this cove is indeed rocky, but the rock
is eroded and faded to a greyish fawn colour and crumbles in parts to a
cindery dust; but the two sides of the cove are masses of black lava,
savage, contorted, split by heat and subsequent cooling into deep fissures
and razor-sharp edges, horrifying and impenetrable. Between these
masses winds up a dusty rocky little valley, colonized by tufts of withered
grass and the indomitable curry-plant, *Helichrysum stoechas*, and, in a
favoured corner, the improbably green leaves of a fig tree. The path winds
up between cone-shaped depressions of fine ash, among scatters of pumice
and heaps of rock, black, reddish and dusted with the bright efflorescence
of sulphur. It is an oppressive scene, every harsh effect is repeated again
and again with the cumulative insistence of nightmare. At the summit, the
latest crater still faintly bubbles and emits puffs of mephitic vapour. It is
as though all the world's slag-heaps and spoil-tips had been combined in
a senseless but menacing composition (plates 9, 10, 11).

It is, then, with a sense of relief that the visitor looks out from a high
place to the great calm circle of deep blue waters around him and the
distant and sunny cliffs of Thera and Therasia, the remote and peaceful
capes of Oea and Akrotiri, the single islet of Aspronisi; and feels a
momentary lifting of the spirits.

Momentary, however, and no more. This savage island on which he is
standing is merely the consequence of a few, relatively minor, eruptions,
spread over the last 200 years; the calm circle of waters, which seemed so
reassuring, is nothing more than the gigantic hole blown in the earth's
surface 3,500 years ago when the ancient island of Stronghyle 'was
swallowed up by the sea and vanished', the sunny cliffs being the torn
sides of the crater.

EIGHT
The Volcanic History of Santorin

During the early period of the fragmentation of the Cycladic land-mass, a small rocky island of phyllites (a rock intermediate between clay-slate and mica-schist) and semi-crystalline limestone, about 15 sq. km in area and quatrefoil in shape, remained in the position of modern Santorin. North-east of this island, about half a mile from the shore, a small isolated reef, the Monolithos of today, broke the surface; and it was in that region of the sea floor that the first volcanic activity took place during the Pliocene. A volcanic cone gradually rose and—in technical terms—the submarine extrusion became a subaerial effusion, the volcanic matter pouring out to form a purely volcanic island. Further extrusions through fissures in the central cone and three other cones enlarged the volcanic island which, in the course of time, was united with the rocky island which was there before any of the eruptions. The island, which was finally formed by the union of lava from a total of seven volcanic centres, was in the shape of an almost perfect circle: hence the original name Stronghyle, which means 'the round one'.

The regularity of its shape must have made Stronghyle attractive in appearance. Its surface was apparently crossed by large ravines. According to H. Reck, before the destructive eruption which produced the first layer of pumice, Santorin was a complicated volcanic mountain whose parts were marked off from one another by very old valleys of great size. According to A. de Lapparent, the submarine valleys which now run between Thera and Therasia and between Therasia and Aspronisi formed

The stages of the volcanic growth of Santorin, around the core provided by Monolithos and Mount Prophet Elias.

large canyons running in those directions, starting from the central cone of Stronghyle and reaching down to the sea. The existence of such ravines is clearly shown in the geological section of the Santorin caldera. In many parts of the caldera, particularly at the points called Perivola, Kato Phera and Athenios (all on the western side of Thera), there are deep ravines filled with more recent loose material, and the width of these ravines is more than 490 ft (150 m) in their upper parts.

The deep weathering of the surface layers of the former island of Stronghyle (which lies under the first layer of pumice) shows that, after the formation of the island there followed a long period of volcanic inactivity. This may likewise be inferred from the violence of the eruption which caused the submersion of the central part of the island. Usually, during a volcanic resting period, the crater is blocked by the cooling of the upper layer of lava, by erosion and by chemical action of the gases in the lava. As a result, the longer a volcano is dormant, the more violent are the eventual eruptions and their accompanying earthquakes.

During Stronghyle's dormancy the weathering of the upper layers had advanced so far that the surface soil of the island was completely sandy to a considerable depth; and the great fertility of this soil, characteristic of all volcanic regions, allowed the pre-eruption inhabitants of Stronghyle to develop a remarkable culture. They were, incidentally, the first known people in the world to use earthquake-resistant methods of construction; and the same kind of earthquake-proof construction is still in use with satisfactory results in many parts of Greece, particularly in the Ionian Islands. C. Paparigopoulos, when describing the life of the prehistoric inhabitants of Stronghyle as deduced from the archaeological findings under the first layer of pumice and ash, writes:

'These people were farmers and fishermen, they had flocks of sheep and goats, they cultivated cereals and ground corn, they produced olive oil, they wove fabrics and used nets in fishing, they had buildings of carved stone and they *inserted pieces of wood in the walls to prevent, as much as possible, the disastrous effects of earthquakes*. They used the potter's wheel to make vessels with strange decorations and original shapes. Most of their tools

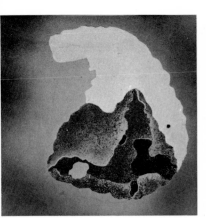 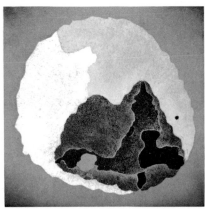 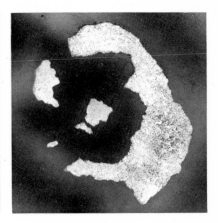

were of stone, the commonest of lava, and others of shaped stone or obsidian. They knew gold and probably copper, although both these metals were rare; above all, timber was plentiful in the island at that time. They communicated with the neighbouring islands as shown by the shape of some of the vases which are similar to those found in Melos, Rhodes and Cyprus.'

After a long period of volcanic quiescence, a tremendous eruption of unparalleled violence put an end to the peace of Stronghyle. As shown by the excavations in Therasia, the people had no time to leave the island or even to take anything from their homes. First came tremendous quantities of pumice, then pumice mixed with ash, sand, lapilli and bombs of every size; and these buried the island with a white shroud, enveloping the inhabitants and all living things. The existence of this shroud can be clearly seen today from the light colour of the ejecta covering the darker lava and scoria of what was once Stronghyle. The thickness of these ejecta, which today form the *pozzolana*, was over 100 ft (30 m) and at some points over 150 ft (45 m); and from the great volume of *pozzolana* now covering the island of Thera it can be inferred that the eruption was of really gigantic proportions.

Pumice is a type of volcanic rock, which is extremely light and porous as the result of a sudden release of steam and gases as it is solidifying. In the eruption pumice and volcanic ash were hurled to a great height and covered the surface of the sea to a great distance around the volcano. Observations made during recent volcanic eruptions have shown that large quantities of pumice floating in a thick layer on the sea must have made navigation very difficult in the Aegean, particularly in the southern parts. Confirmation of this comes from several sources. Professor Marinatos has found a thick layer of pumice at Amnisos, the port of Minoan Knossos, in Crete. Volcanic ash, most probably from the Stronghyle eruption, was found south of Crete in 1947–8 in sediment cores taken by the Swedish expedition ship *Albatros*. Professor Max Pfannenstiel found layers of sea-borne pumice in sediments of a post-glacial terrace 16½ ft (5 m) above sea-level, north of Jaffa–Tel Aviv. According to Pfannenstiel these layers come from the Santorin eruption.

After the magmatic chamber was emptied by the pouring out of such vast quantities of materials, a cavity of huge dimensions was formed under the central part of the island of Stronghyle. Owing to the cavity's size, the roof collapsed and the sea water rushed into the hollow.

The water, suddenly striking the bottom of the cavity, violently recoiled. The sudden movement of such huge quantities of sea water created sea waves of prodigious height. These waves, spreading in all directions, flooded the coasts of the eastern Mediterranean to a great height above sea-level, completely devastating all towns and settlements in and round the Aegean.

According to Professor R. W. Hutchinson, of the larger settlements in

Pumice floating on the sea during the eruption of Surtsey in 1963. The Santorin eruption must have thrown out much greater quantities of pumice, which would have impeded shipping considerably, recalling Plato's description of the ocean becoming 'impassable and unsearchable, being blocked up by the shoal mud which the island created as it settled down'.

the lowlands of Crete only Palaikastro and Zakro in the far east seem 'to have escaped from the worst effects of the floods and earthquakes', which probably initiated and accompanied the collapse of the central part of Stronghyle. (Recent excavations at both these sites indicate that they likewise suffered catastrophically.) The distribution of damage throughout Crete, as suggested by the archaeological evidence, provides a fairly strong clue to the origins of the Minoan collapse in the fifteenth century BC.

A faint idea of the destructive power of the gigantic waves which followed the collapse of the central part of Stronghyle may be reached by a calculation of their height. The amplitude of a *tsunami* is proportionate to the initial amplitude and inversely proportionate to the square root of the distance the wave has travelled. In addition to the loss of amplitude due to the wave's spreading out, there is also a certain loss from absorption due to frictional dissipation of the elastic energy into heat. Assuming an eustatic rise of the sea-level by 6 or 9 ft in the time interval of about 3,500 years, the height of the sea waves in Jaffa–Tel Aviv should have been at least 22 ft. Disregarding now the loss from absorption and taking into account that the sea waves produced by the collapse of Stronghyle had a height of more than 22 ft (7 m) when they reached Jaffa–Tel Aviv, about 562 miles (900 km) away, we can easily calculate that their height at starting point would be at least 690 ft (210 m). This calculation of the initial height of the *tsunami* is in accordance with Professor Marinos' recent estimate.

Interesting and illuminating effects have been found on the island of Anaphi, which lies about 15 miles (24 km) east of Santorin. Here Professor Marinos and his collaborator, N. Melidonis, found layers of pumice in three places. On the western side (that facing Santorin) they found a layer of thick-grained pumice mixed with pieces of 4–6 in. (10–15 cm) diameter; and this was 385 yds (350 m) from the coast and between 130 and 170 ft (40–50 m) above sea-level. The two other deposits are on the north-east side of the island, the side away from Santorin. The first of these is at a height of 530 ft (160 m) above sea-level and 820 yds (750 m) from the sea; while the second is about a mile (1,650 m) from the coast and 820 ft (250 m) above sea-level. All three layers of pumice were found at the heads of ravines or valleys.

According to Marinos and Melidonis, this pumice was deposited by the sea waves which followed the formation of the volcanic cavity of Santorin. If it had been carried by the wind, these writers state, it would have been found in the interior of the island where it would have been better pre-served in level and sheltered locations than was the case in the sloping sites where it was actually found. The fact that the pumice was found at a greater height on the north-east coast of Anaphi than on the western, Santorin-facing, coast can be accounted for by the eastern barrier of the Island of Thera, the north-west direction of the deepest channel through which the water spread out from the caldera, and the convergence of the waves sweeping round the island. A parallel to this can be found in the *tsunami* which started from Chile on 23 May 1960. This reached a height of 17 ft on the south-eastern side of Hawaii—the coast, that is, which directly faced the direction of the *tsunami*; whereas, on the north-eastern side, near the town of Hilo, it reached a height of 35 ft above sea-level, and even on the north-western shores touched the height of 20 ft.

Other examples of the height reached by *tsunamis* are as follows. In the Kamchatka peninsula, in 1937, a *tsunami* was 210 ft high. In Norway in 1936, a landslide in Lake Loen caused a 230-ft wave. In Italy, on 6 February 1873, a landslide-generated wave swept three miles inland at Scilla. Finally, and more recently, in the Alaska earthquake of July 1958 a giant wave, observed on the south coast of Lituya Bay, reached a height of 680 ft, while on the north coast the waters rose to 1,720 ft.

The classic example of the destructive effects of a sea-wave is to be found in the *tsunami* which struck the north-east coast of the Japanese island of Hondo on 16 June 1896. In the course of five minutes this wave destroyed 7,600 houses; 27,000 people lost their lives and 5,000 were injured; 18 boats and sailing ships and a vessel of 200 tons were hurled more than 490 yds (450 m) inland from the coast. The *tsunami* which followed the eastern Mediterranean earthquake of 21 July AD 365 carried a ship 1¼ miles (2 km) inland near Methoni on the south coast of the Peloponnese. The same wave struck Egypt and in the harbour of Alexandria lifted ships over the waterfront houses and deposited them in the streets behind. In more recent times (9 July 1956) the *tsunami* which followed the Amorgos earthquake in the Aegean was observed in Palestine. This wave, which started from the tectonic trench between the islands of Amorgos and Astypalaea, reached a height of 82 ft (25 m) on the south coast of Amorgos and of 65 ft (20 m) on the north coast of Astypalaea. At the island of Ios it was 29½ ft (8 m) high. It caused considerable damage to the islands of Calymnos, Leros, Sikinos, Nissyros and Karpathos, besides the three already mentioned; while lesser damage was reported in Crete, Patmos, Ikaria, Tilos, Alymia, Melos, Seriphos, Antiparos and Tenos. Over 80 boats and small vessels were destroyed; but the only human casualty was an old woman, who was drowned.

The combined effects of water and pumice are well illustrated in a submarine eruption at Coloumbos, outside the great caldera of Santorin and about 4 miles (6·5 km) north-east of the promontory of the same name. The volcanic phenomena started on 14 September 1650 with frequent earthquakes, night and day. On 26 September, after a violent earthquake, a volcanic cone appeared above the surface of the sea. The major eruption took place on 29 September and it was accompanied by a violent earthquake and a huge *tsunami* which swept over the east coast of Thera for a distance of 2 miles, filling all the valleys with pebbles and dead fish. On the island of Ios (about 20 miles away) the waves rose to 50 ft and at Sikinos the *tsunami* swept 350 ft inland. At Kea a ship was hurled on shore. In Crete many ships were torn from their moorings and some sank in the harbour of Heraklion. In Patmos it was reported that the sea rose 164 ft (50 m) and 98 ft (30 m) on the west and east coasts respectively. A curious effect observed in Thera, after the withdrawal of the sea water, was that the remains of the ancient towns at Kamari and Perissa were temporarily uncovered. These two small towns lie on the south-east coast of Thera on either side of the Mesa Vouno promontory. When the ancient towns were originally submerged is not yet known.

Many houses in Thera were damaged and the mountain called Merovigli was split. The sound of the submarine eruption could be heard in Chios about 140 miles (224 km) away and the volcanic ash was carried by the wind to Asia Minor, where it was said to cover the leaves of trees with a whitish film.

The phenomena of the Coloumbos eruption lasted three months. Poisonous gases close to the shore killed 40 peasants and a large number of animals, the plain being covered with dead birds and other animals. Many of the inhabitants lost their sight for six to eight days. Hydrogen sulphide fumes tarnished silver and gold coins and other articles, even those enclosed in boxes. A sailing ship near Coloumbos was immobilized in floating pumice and the crew of nine met a sudden and tragic death. The pumice was so thick on the sea that it supported stones thrown on to it, and it was believed by many to be thick enough to support a man walking or lying on it. It was so extensive as to cover the sea among the Cyclades group of islands. After a short time the volcanic island formed by the eruption disappeared below the waves, and the top of the cone is now 10 fathoms (18·5 m) below the surface of the sea.

The way, however, to appreciate the scale of the tragic events which followed the prodigious eruption of Stronghyle–Santorin in the fifteenth century BC is to compare it with the eruption of Krakatoa, the greatest ever recorded in historical times, which took place on 27 August 1883. According to the German volcanologist, H. Reck, the basin-shaped volcanic cavity or caldera of Santorin was formed in the same way as the volcanic depression at Krakatoa, in the Strait of Sunda, between Sumatra and Java.

The Krakatoa eruption occurred after the volcano had been dormant for 203 years. It began on 20 May 1883, but the explosive activity (plate 24) was mild and intermittent until the climax was reached on 27 August. Then, after the culminating explosions, two-thirds of the island (whose area was 21 sq. miles (33½ sq. km)) collapsed and a crater-like cavity 110–160 fathoms (200–300 m) deep was formed. The waters of the Indian Ocean rushed into the cavity. This sudden shift of such large quantities of water produced three huge waves. At Anjer in Java these reached a height of 118 ft (36 m); and at Telukbetung, in Sumatra, 131 ft (40 m). At Telukbetung a Dutch warship was washed ashore and left stranded half a mile inland and 30 ft above sea-level. Anjer and 29 other towns on the neighbouring coasts of Java and Sumatra were wholly or partly destroyed and 36,000 people were killed or drowned. The atmospheric waves generated by the Krakatoa eruption jumped over the land barriers and re-excited sea waves strong enough to break the anchor chains of ships moored in the port of Valparaiso, Chile. It was estimated 'that a surface explosion amounting to about 100–150 megatons would produce pressure pulses equivalent to those observed from Krakatoa'.

The sound of the eruption was so loud that window panes were smashed and walls cracked 100 miles (160 km) away. It was heard 2,250 miles to the south-east—in Australia—and 2,968 miles to the west in the Indian Ocean island of Rodriguez. The sound waves travelled three times round the world. For many miles round the island the floating pumice was 13 ft (4 m) thick. The volcanic ash was hurled to a height of 15–18½ miles (25–30 km); and the quantity of the ash was so great that it darkened the sky for 275 miles (440 km) around, turning day into night. At a distance of 130 miles the darkness lasted for 22 hours, and within a radius of 50 miles for 57 hours. Three days after the eruption huge quantities of ash fell on the decks of vessels 1,600 miles away. Deep channels filled up with volcanic material and were no longer navigable. At the climax of the eruption fine volcanic dust rose to a height of 50 miles (80 km) and part of it fell in Japan, Africa and Europe. Owing to the reflection of sunlight from the dust particles in the upper atmosphere, 'sun glows' appeared in the sky and 'fire engines were summoned at Poughkeepsie (New York) and New Haven (Connecticut) to quench the burning skies'. The brilliant glow in the skies continued to appear, before sunrise and after sunset, all over Europe and the United States, with varying brilliance for months.

It has been computed that the total volume of material extruded by the eruption was about 11 cu. miles (18 cu. km). Together with this material were 3 cu. miles of gases under an original pressure of 425 atmospheres, at a temperature of 1,400°C. The thermal energy of the main eruption was equivalent to 100,000 million kilowatt hours; while the total energy of the eruption has been calculated at 200 million millions of kilowatt hours. The total consumption of electric energy all over the world in 1950 was 250 times less than the total thermal energy of the 1883 eruption of Krakatoa.

Let us now compare the result of two great volcanic eruptions—that of Krakatoa in AD 1883, and that of Santorin in the fifteenth century BC. The Santorin caldera is 32 sq. miles (83 sq. km) in surface and 160-220 fathoms (300-400 m) deep. The Krakatoa caldera does not exceed 8 sq. miles (22 sq. km) in area and 110-160 fathoms (200-300 m) in depth. The Santorin caldera is therefore about five times greater in volume than that of Krakatoa. The thickness of the ash thrown out at Krakatoa does not exceed 16 in. (40 cm). The ash-covered area at Santorin is much greater and the thickness of the layer reaches 100-130 ft (30-40 m).

The thermal energy produced at the Santorin eruption, according to Peter Hédervári, was about three times that of the corresponding energy of Krakatoa. The energy of the *tsunami* produced by the collapse of the subterranean cavity after the magma was extruded at Santorin was at least half the energy of that observed after the Chile earthquake of May 1960. The effects of the Chilean *tsunami* were disastrous on the coasts of Japan 10,625 miles (17,000 km) away from the source of the wave. The greatest damage was observed in the districts of Tohoku and Hokkaido. In Hirota Bay the wave was 19½ ft (6 m) high. In Hawaii, 6,250 miles (10,000 km) from its source, the *tsunami* caused 61 deaths and material damage of about $20,000,000.

We have, therefore, fully attested knowledge of the cataclysmic effects of two modern disasters: the eruption of Krakatoa in 1883 and the Chilean earthquake *tsunami* of 1960. We know also from the surviving evidence of Santorin that the thermal energy of its explosion was about three times that of Krakatoa and the *tsunami* energy at least half that of the Chilean *tsunami*. There cannot be a shadow of doubt that the Santorin eruption was truly prodigious in scale. Occurring in the middle of the Aegean, a relatively densely populated centre of Bronze Age civilization, it could hardly have been forgotten and must surely have been preserved in tradition. Two aspects of it are of particular importance: first, no other submersion of an inhabited land occurred to such an extent, to such a depth, or so suddenly; second, that we have indisputable proof that the disaster actually occurred.

As described previously, Santorin today strikes even the casual visitor with awe. Even without any knowledge of geology, as he looks up from the centre of the harbour at the inner sides of the caldera rising up to some 1,150 ft (350 m) above sea level, there can be no doubt in his mind that this was the result of the collapse of the middle of a large, round island. If he then recalls that the sea-bed is much the same depth below him as the top of the cliffs are above him, the gigantic scale and horror of this collapse will strike him even more forcibly. The arrangement of clearly distinct levels of lava at the same height and in the same order in the three islands, Thera, Therasia and Aspronisi, which, wreath-like, encircle the elliptical abyss which lies among them, demonstrates that these multicoloured and precipitous walls—laid bare like geological sections—are the interior of one single, original island.

This colossal piece of nature's architecture was created, then, in a single cataclysm, which took place in the fifteenth century BC. What is its later volcanic history? The eruption of Coloumbos in AD 1650 has already been described—but this took place outside the caldera and has in any case left no immediately visible traces.

Inside the caldera, however, are two islands, which are the fusion of a number of volcanic cones thrown up from the bottom of the caldera. After the great cataclysm there was a period of quiescence lasting some 1,300 years. Then in 198 BC a volcanic island was thrown up and called Hiera; in AD 46 another eruption, about 400 yds (370 m) away, created another island, named Theia; and in AD 60 a third eruption completely united the two islands. In AD 726 a fourth eruption increased the size of the island created by the union of Hiera and Theia. Incidentally, great quantities of pumice were thrown out on this occasion and floating pumice reached Asia Minor, Lesbos, Abydos and the Macedonian coast. After this there was a period of quiescence of 731 years. In AD 1457 and 1508 further eruptions increased the size of this island; but there has been no further activity in this island, which reached its present shape at this point. It is now called Palaea (Old) Kameni and its highest point is about 330 ft (110 m) above sea level.

In AD 1573, that is, 65 years after Palaea Kameni reached its present form, activity broke out some 2,600 yds (2,400 m) north-east of the centre of Palaea Kameni and a small oval island (500 × 300 m) came into being. This was called Mikra (Small) Kameni. (In 1650 the Couloumbos eruption took place outside the caldera.) In 1707 volcanic activity started again, this time some 217 yds (200 m) west of Small Kameni. Two volcanic cones appeared and were named Aspronisi and Macronesi. These were united in the course of five years to form a third islet, between Old and Small Kameni, larger and higher than either, and named Nea (New) Kameni.

In 1866 fresh activity broke out and in the course of four years, three

The eruption of the Kameni islands in 1866, from a contemporary engraving (*top right*). The eruption continued into 1867, when this rare and early photograph (*right*) was taken.

The eruption of Nea Kameni in 1950.

Renewed activity of the Kameni volcano in 1870, from contemporary engravings (*left*). The upper picture shows the approach to the Santorin lagoon from the north-west; in the distance are the walls of the caldera, and Mount Prophet Elias.

new volcanic cones—Georgios, Aphroessa and Reka—appeared and almost quadrupled the size of Nea Kameni. The activity began in a small bay on the south-east coast of Nea Kameni, then known as Vulcanos, and the cone Georgios, which appeared at this point, is today the highest point of the Kameni group. During the 1886 eruption a fall of rain was observed, caused by the condensation of the steam emitted by the volcano.

The most recent major eruption took place sixty years later, in 1925 between New and Small Kameni, in a small bay known as Kokkina Nera. A small islet appeared in this bay and was called Daphne. It rapidly increased in size as the result of large lava flows and united Small and New Kameni. Eruptions in 1928, 1939-41 and 1956 have increased the amount of lava without appreciably altering the size of the present island, now known as Nea Kameni.

The volcanic history of Santorin since the great collapse is well known and well documented and the manner and dates of the changes are established. What can be established about the date or dates of the great eruption and the collapse?

It is quite clear that the caving in of the central portion occurred after the volcanic paroxysm and after colossal quantities of pumice had been extruded. When the visitor examines the cliff-walls of the caldera, he sees immediately that the two layers of *pozzolana* have been cut off in exactly the same way as the layers of lava and scoria on which they rest, i.e. they were already deposited before the collapse took place (plates 9, 13).

During excavations in Thera and Therasia, houses of the prehistoric inhabitants were found under the first rose-coloured layer of pumice which covered the whole surface of Stronghyle; and the walls of these houses were still standing. This led Reck to argue that earthquakes strong enough to cause damage did not occur before, during or after the volcanic paroxysm in Santorin. This was probably true only for the first phase of the eruption—that which produced the first layer of pumice which covered the houses of the islanders. The collapse of the cavity (created after the magma chamber had been emptied) occurred after the *pozzolana* had been deposited, as Reck has proved. Therefore, earthquakes accompanying the collapse, no matter how great they might have been, could not possibly have demolished walls which were already packed or boxed in with a thick layer of pumice and volcanic ash.

As regards the date of these occurrences, Professor Sp. Marinatos,

PLATE 13. The Akrotiri peninsula, the southern part of the island of Thera and area of recent excavations (*top right*). In this photograph the successive strata of lava and *pozzolana* can be seen very clearly. *Bottom right* Part of the excavation site at Akrotiri. In the distance can be seen the islands of Aspronisi (left) and Therasia.

Human teeth discovered in a *pozzolana* quarry near Phera in 1956. Two of them are burnt, which suggests that the volcanic ash was still extremely hot when it buried the owners of the teeth.

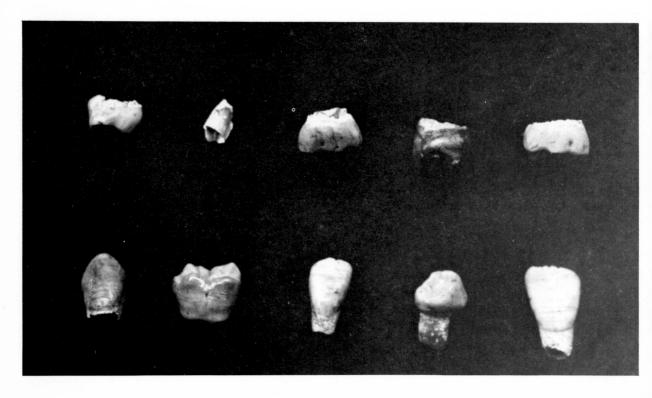

arguing from archaeological findings in Santorin and the thick layer of pumice found in Crete, believes that the coastal settlements of Crete were destroyed by the *tsunami* which followed the submersion of the central part of Santorin, at a date which he puts at about 1520 BC.

After the destructive Santorin earthquake of 9 July 1956, one of us (A.G.) visited Thera to assess the damage caused by it and was informed by Mr C. Papageorgiou, the owner of a *pozzolana* quarry, that there were prehistoric relics under the lowest layer of pumice. This quarry is near Phera, the capital of Thera. In a prehistoric wall were found various fragments of pottery, some stone tools, human bones and teeth (two of them burnt), olive leaves and charred pieces of pine. The pieces of wood were immediately sent to the Lamont Geological Observatory, Columbia University, N.Y. Radiocarbon measurements by F. A. Olson and W.S. Broecker proved that the samples sent died—that is, were removed from the carbon dioxide cycle by ceasing to be living plants—$3,370 \pm 100$ years ago, i.e. not earlier than 1510 BC and not later than 1310 BC. This dating does not conflict with the dates based on the pottery and wall-paintings found on Crete.

Recently J. G. Bennett, taking into consideration the chronology of the flood of Deucalion as inferred from the famous Parian marble, and the date of the death of the Pharaoh Tuthmosis III at the time of the Exodus of the Israelites, suggested that the submersion of the central part of Santorin took place in 1447 BC—a date consonant with the radiocarbon findings.

This radiocarbon date ($3370 - 1960 = 1410 \pm 100$ BC) referred to the time the first layer of *pozzolana* was deposited and not to the time the caldera was formed. This latter event took place after the whole layer of *pozzolana* was deposited. It is almost certain that some years, if not decades, were required for a layer of pumice and volcanic ash to be formed to a depth of 100–130 ft (30–40 m). Taking into account the fact that the ash thrown out at Krakatoa during the course of three months did not exceed 40 cm, and assuming the same rate of deposition in Santorin, we might conclude that the eruption of the Santorin volcano lasted about 25 years. In addition, after the first, or rose-coloured pumice, eruption the volcano was for a time quiescent. Again, on the top of the middle pumice layer, which is $16\frac{1}{2}$–33 ft (5–10 m) thick, there are some traces of erosion, which would indicate a second period of quiescence for the volcano. Furthermore, the pieces of wood, found below the first layer of pumice, may have been removed from the carbon dioxide cycle, that is, cut and used some years before the eruption. Thus the collapse of the central part of the island—which took place after the deposition of three distinct layers of pumice and volcanic ash—may have been at least 20–30 years later than the date found by the radiocarbon method.

We have reached, by logical and scientific methods, a number of conclusions.

The island of Stronghyle, whose remains are called Santorin, was the

PLATE 14. Another view of the excavation site at Akrotiri. 'To the uninstructed eye, all that appears is a number of fragmentary stone walls deep in a landscape of volcanic dust.'

scene of a cataclysmic volcanic eruption, followed by the collapse of the whole interior of the island, with consequent *tsunamis* or sea-waves.

Within a few years of the onset of this disaster, pieces of wood were cut from a tree and survived the years buried under deep layers of pumice. Radiocarbon dating establishes that these pieces of wood were cut from the tree at a date, within 100 years (more or less) of 1410 BC, i.e. between 1510 and 1310 BC. Therefore the tree could not have been living before, say, 1540 and certainly not after 1310 BC.

Further, after the cutting of this tree, there followed a period, which may have been as long as 20 or 30 years, during which there were three distinct eruptions, each with an enormous production of pumice; and these eruptions were followed by the disappearance of the whole centre of the island in a vast collapse producing a sea-wave without parallel which must have had disastrous effects on the Aegean and Eastern Mediterranean coasts.

Section 4

CASE PROVEN

NINE
Ancient Metropolis and Royal City

We have now reached a point at which the evidence so far uncovered may well be summarized, when the solution is in sight and where such anomalies as still remain can be considered.

The case, so far, is as follows. We accept that Plato's story is history rather than fiction or parable. We show that on internal evidence the events of this story must have taken place in the Bronze Age, i.e. between 2100 and 1200 BC. We have established that the Ancient Metropolis and the Royal City are two separate places, the former being a small round island of about $5\frac{3}{4}$ miles (9·5 km) in radius, the latter an oblong area, much larger, and possibly very large indeed. We have shown that it is not geophysically possible for Atlantis to have been located in the Atlantic; and proved that none of the theories so far advanced to account for its sudden submersion are tenable. We have gone on to indicate that the only logical location must be in the Eastern Mediterranean and that the identification of the Pillars of Hercules with the Straits of Gibraltar need not be taken too literally. Finally, we have shown that volcanic activity on a really stupendous scale did take place in the Eastern Mediterranean in the middle of the Bronze Age, that this activity was centred on the island of Santorin, and that it resulted in, among other things, the sudden disappearance of the whole centre of an inhabited, small, round island.

The case, therefore, for the identification of Santorin with the Ancient Metropolis of Atlantis is extremely strong, and is supported by a considerable amount of corroborative evidence of very great interest.

Plato does not actually say that the Metropolis was built on a volcano; but his description clearly suggests a small volcanic island after a long period of volcanic repose. He states that the acropolis was built on a small hill in the centre of the island near a fertile plain, the best in the world, by his description; and it is a fact that the most fertile soils are volcanic soils, weathered during a long period of volcanic inactivity. In describing the buildings, moreover, he refers to stones coloured black, red and white. Red, and especially black, rocks are characteristic of volcanic regions; and in Thera, the largest island of Santorin and the largest remaining part of Stronghyle–Santorin, there are red, black and white rocks, the last being the limestones round Mount Prophet Elias, the original pre-volcanic island round which the rest of the complex came into being.

Elsewhere in the account Plato mentions cold and hot springs. Warm springs are met with only in volcanic regions and are in fact characteristic of such regions. In Stronghyle–Santorin there must have been such springs. A report by V. Acylas confirms this view. He writes: 'When in June 1923 I visited the crater known as Georgios [now part of Nea Kameni] where hot sulphurous gases were there exhaled, particularly sulphuric acid, with a deposit of sulphur crystals in the fissures round the crater, I entered by boat the elongated little bay and landed at its head. I noticed that in the bay, in the direction of New Kameni, close to where there were some half-submerged huts of New Kameni, there was an underwater spring of warm water, evidently with a strong solution of iron salts which coloured the bay a vivid red colour. The bay was known as Ta Kokkina Nera (the red waters).'

There was formerly a hot spring on the south-east coast of New Kameni at the point of the bay called Vulcanos. According to A. Christomanos, this spring, which was quite plentiful and poured into the sea, had a temperature of $25\,^\circ$C ($77\,^\circ$F) in 1864. The proportion of iron and hydrogen sulphide that the spring contained was so high that the inhabitants of Thera used the bay as a spa. Acylas adds: 'It was enough for ships to enter and stay for some hours in this small bay for the copper bottoms of the ships to become clean and bright under the influence of the salts in solution in the sea water.' The 'red waters', which used to lie between Small and New Kameni at the point where the cone called Daphne emerged in 1925, had the same qualities. Even today in the little bay on the north side of New Kameni, where visitors land when visiting the volcano, the waters are curiously mixed in temperature, as is immediately apparent when one bathes there and swims out of cold water into warm and back into cold again. The water also smells sulphurous.

As regards the existence of cold freshwater springs on ancient Santorin, the evidence, both direct and indirect, is satisfactory. To this day there is an excellent spring of fresh water, called Zoodochos, in the original pre-volcanic limestone above Kamari. It is known that the ancient vegetation of the island included palms, lentisk and olive (*Phoenix dactylifera, Chamaerops humilis, Pistacia lentiscus* and *Olea europea*). To quote Julius Schuster, who has studied this flora; 'As the Chamaerops implies moist bush, there is no need to think of a more humid climate. Probably there were springs in the neighbourhood of this vegetation.' In addition H. Reck, the German volcanologist, argues that before the cataclysm the now-submerged area on either side of the islet of Aspronisi, between the southernmost points of Thera and Therasia, was a low-lying and fertile plain. Ancient settlements have been found on either side of this area, which was almost certainly the source of the clay from which the local pottery was made. Clay does not outcrop in Santorin today, but the ancient pottery found does contain chips of Thera lava. This clay could well have come from the fresh or salt water lakes which might be expected in what Reck calls the plain of Aspronisi.

Plato's description of the structure and shape of the Ancient Metropolis is consistent with the acropolis being built on the central cone of Stronghyle–Santorin; and, as can be seen most clearly in the diagram, the dimensions of Santorin and the Ancient Metropolis are of the same order of magnitude.

More than forty years ago Professor John Trikkalinos (a former President of the Athens Academy, but then working as an assistant at the Geological Laboratory) made a relief model of the Santorin caldera, the Kameni island-group and the islands of Thera, Therasia and Aspronisi based on the British Admiralty chart of 1916. This model (plate 3) is today in the Geological Museum of Athens. (The model was made before the eruption of 1925 which united the islands of Nea and Mikra Kameni, but otherwise represents the present shape and structure of Santorin.) In this model traces of the harbours of the Ancient Metropolis and of the canal joining them with the sea can be distinguished without difficulty. The traces of the harbours are quite clear between Nea Kameni and the town of Phera and particularly so between Palaea and Nea Kameni, where the circular shape of the central harbour can be seen.

In the illustration the Atlantis Metropolis, as described by Plato, has been superimposed on a sketch map of Santorin, on the same scale. If this figure is compared with the model, one can see that the traces of the channels on the bottom of the caldera have the same width as the sea-zones described by Plato and that their distance from the central volcanic cone is precisely the same as the distance of the corresponding sea-zones from the hill which carried the Temple of Poseidon. There is a discrepancy in Plato's description. In *Critias 113C* the acropolis is on a small hill 50 stades from the sea; in *Critias 117E*, however, the outer zone encircling the acropolis is 50 stades from the sea. The diagram is based on the second passage. If, however, it is the first passage which is correct, the radius of the Ancient Metropolis must have been $1\frac{1}{4}$ miles (2 km) smaller than that shown in the diagram and would therefore correspond almost exactly with the radius of Santorin today, and, moreover, the length of the submarine gorge which lies between Thera and Therasia would be exactly the same as the length of the channel joining the sea with the inner harbour of the Ancient Metropolis.

This coincidence is indeed remarkable, but even more striking is the shape of the sea-mouth of the submarine gorge. Plato records that the inhabitants of Atlantis had widened the mouth of the channel to allow the biggest ships of the time to sail into the harbour. It could perhaps be admitted that the traces of the harbours on the caldera floor might be a coincidence resulting from its morphological features; but it is extremely difficult to accept the same explanation of the clearly defined entrance to the underwater gorge between Thera and Therasia. Its shape and depth preclude its formation by erosion; and these, together with the coincidence of the length of the underwater gorge and of the connecting channel of Atlantis, are strong arguments against the contention that the traces in general are the result of simple coincidence. The coincidences, in fact, are too many and too strong to be accepted as accidental.

From Plato's description it is apparent that the zones of sea were—at least, in the main—natural channels surrounding the central cone. On the other hand the canal joining these belts of water with the sea was man-made for at least part of its length. The zones of sea round the hill were credited to Poseidon (the god, incidentally, of earthquakes) at a time when there were no such things as ships (*Crit.*, *113D–E*). These belts of water, says Plato, contained sea-water, and were therefore, it would appear, in communication with the sea; but presumably this connection was insufficient for ships to pass, since the descendants of Poseidon are described by Plato (*Crit.*, *115C–E*) as making the channel wide enough for a single trireme to sail right in; and also as covering over this sea-channel and making it subterranean.

The distinction between the natural circular channels and the largely man-made canal joining these circles with the sea solves to some extent the problem of how so many harbours were made in a region consisting mainly of tuff and andesite lava. After massive eruptions which deplete the magma chamber, broad tracts surrounding the volcano often subside,

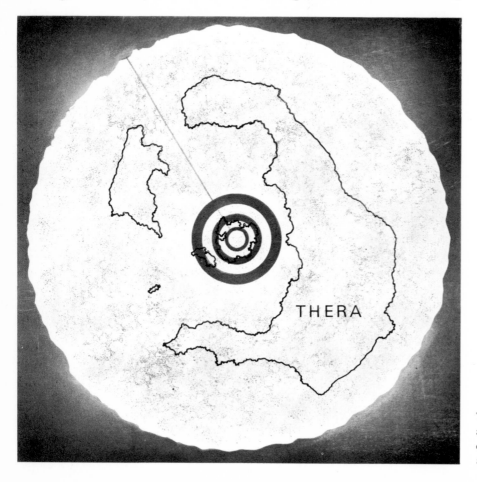

The relative sizes of Santorin and of the Ancient Metropolis of Atlantis, based on Plato's account in the *Critias*.

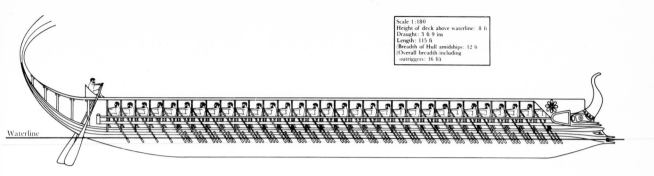

Waterline

Reconstruction drawing of a Greek trireme, the kind of ship described by Plato in his account of the channel that connected the Metropolis of Atlantis with the sea.

and these subsidences, if near sea level, may be inundated. As previously mentioned, the surface of Stronghyle–Santorin was traversed by steep gorges of considerable depth and breadth and the bottom of these gorges was below sea-level. According to Reck, in the central position of the present caldera there was a dome-like height of medium altitude surrounded by isolated hills. Other investigators believe that this height was surrounded by ring-like valleys. In such conditions the shaping of these valleys would not have presented insurmountable difficulties at that time, if one takes into consideration the weathering of the lava (which must have advanced to a considerable depth) and the astonishing feats of civil engineering of which ancient man was capable.

In the Second Millennium BC—the presumed era of Atlantis—the laws of natural selection were in full sway among mankind. Out of each generation only the hardiest survived; thousands of slaves worked for the comfort of the few and their labour was cheap and expendable. In such circumstances incredible achievements became possible with even the minimum of technological achievements, and in many cases the surviving evidence shows that technical knowledge must have been high.

It is perhaps sufficient to mention the so-called Treasury of Atreus at Mycenae, the vast megalithic constructions at Stonehenge and at Carnac in Western France and, in the New World, at a later but comparable era, the buildings of Cuzco in Peru. But even more convincing and less well-known is the Tunnel of Eupalinos in the island of Samos. This is a monumental aqueduct, constructed in the middle of the sixth century BC on the instructions of the tyrant Polycrates of Samos by the engineer Eupalinos of Megara. It consists of a tunnel 1,093 yards (1,000 m) in length, passing through Mount Speliani, which consists of granite, and its walls are perfectly vertical. The height of the tunnel varies from 4 ft 10 in. to 6 ft 3 in. (1·45–1·9 m) and its width from 7 ft 7 in. to 7 ft 11 in. (2·3–2·4 m). Along its floor runs a channel about 24 in. (60 cm) in width. The depth of this channel is 8 ft 4 in. (2·53 m) at the north entrance, 16 ft 1 in. (4·90 m) in the middle, and 27 ft 1 in. (8·25 m) at the southern exit. The sides of the channel are perfectly vertical and equidistant throughout its length—and it is carved out of granite. In this channel were pipes bringing water to the city of Samos from the spring Aghiades on the further side of Mount Speliani.

The map shows locations in Crete: White Mountains, Herakleion, Amnisos, Pseira, Tylissos, Knossos, Mallia, Palaïkastro, Mt Ida, Mt Juktas, Plain of Messara, Mt Dikte, Kato Zakro, Phaistos, Koumasa.

The island of Crete, showing the principal Minoan sites. The plain of Messara is possibly the plain of the Royal City of Atlantis described by Plato.

It is worth while pausing to consider the magnitude of this achievement in terms of skill and labour—carried through, it must be remembered, without machinery or explosives; and to reflect that it is unwise to underrate the civil engineering potential of antiquity.

Therefore Stronghyle–Santorin, besides being in the right place and suffering the right sort of cataclysm at the right time in history, also has even today a number of the right physical features, surprising in view of its natural vicissitudes, to equate it with the Ancient Metropolis of Atlantis.

But what of the Royal City? It is quite clear from Plato's account that the Ancient Metropolis and the Royal City with its associated plains and mountains are two quite distinct places.

Is there any area reasonably near Santorin which likewise suffered a disastrous cataclysm at the same time in history? Disregarding for the moment the enormous size which Plato indicates, there is in all other respects an obvious answer—Crete. From the description of the features and shape of the plain surrounding the Royal City, it is evident that it possessed the geological characteristics of the strata that form the Tertiary basin of central Crete. This basin is in the middle of the island and is surrounded by mountains reaching to the sea—mountains which have all the characteristics of those that surrounded the plain of the Royal City. In them lie fertile villages and it is certain that in antiquity the vegetation was much denser and that the mountains would be covered in forest. In particular the plain of Messara is very similar to the description of the

The Treasury of Atreus at Mycenae, one of the great buildings of the Bronze Age in Greece.

plain of the Royal City: it is oblong, level, on the south side of the island and sheltered from the north winds—in fact and in sum it agrees as well as could be expected with the plain of the Royal City (plate 18).

But the dimensions of this central basin of Crete do not tally with those which Plato gives for the plain of the Royal City. The greatest length of the basin is 34 miles (54 km) and its breadth is 23 miles (37 km)—in other words, almost exactly 300 stades by 200 stades. Plato, however, gave the length and breadth of the plain of the Royal City as 3,000 and 2,000 stades, adding that it was surrounded by a trench 10,000 stades in length. He goes on to state that he does not believe that men could dig a ditch of

Solon, one of the Seven Sages of Greece, who is represented in Plato's *Timaeus* and *Critias* as having brought the Atlantis story from Egypt. This Roman portrait bust is a copy of a Greek original in the style of the fourth century BC. Though not to be taken as an authentic likeness of Solon, who lived before the earliest individual portraits of the Greeks, the bust indicates how Greeks of Plato's time envisaged 'the wisest of the Seven'.

such length; and in fact the first doubts to arise in Plato's mind about the truth of the story arise from these dimensions. He must have sensed that there was an error, but, lacking other evidence and bearing in mind the seemingly reliable origin of the story, says that he has given the account exactly as he heard it.

When we compare the dimensions of the central plain of Crete with those of the plain of the Royal City, we are immediately aware that the dimensions given for the latter are just ten times too large—the figures have been multiplied by the factor 10. The same mistake appears in the extent and number of allotments, the chariots and ships, in the distances of the canals in the plain as well as in the length of the trench which surrounds the plain. Moreover, exactly the same mistake is evident in the date given by Plato for the submersion of Atlantis. According to the priests of Sais, Atlantis was submerged 9,000 years before Solon's visit to Egypt. Now we have already shown, on cultural grounds, that the empire and submersion of Atlantis could not have been earlier than the Bronze Age. On geophysical grounds we know that during the Bronze Age there was no sudden submersion of an inhabited piece of land comparable with the submersion that we know happened in the Eastern Mediterranean around 1500 BC; and we have shown that the devastation on the shores of the Aegean around that date must have been unparalleled in the history of mankind. It is impossible that such a disaster should not be preserved in tradition; and it would have been strange indeed if tradition should preserve events much less sensational and forget an unprecedented catastrophe that took place in the middle of the Aegean during the highest peak of the Minoan and Helladic civilizations.

Solon, who was born in 639 and died in 559 BC, must have visited Egypt in about 600 BC. Since the collapse of the central part of the island of Stronghyle–Santorin and the devastation of the eastern Mediterranean shores undoubtedly happened around 1500 BC, it is evident that the Atlantis story refers to a geological event which took place 900 years and not 9,000 years before Solon's visit to Egypt. The figure for the date of the submersion of Atlantis is, therefore, ten times greater than it should be. This leads us to the inevitable conclusion that the mistakes in the date of the Atlantis catastrophe and in the dimensions of the plain of the Royal City are systematic and not accidental; and arise in the same way.

The dimensions Plato gives for the Ancient Metropolis are, however, in agreement with the dimensions of Stronghyle–Santorin; but this shows that when dimensions are given in units of tens of stades they are quite correct. When, however, dimensions and dates are given in thousands they are all ten times too great. This seems to indicate that when Solon was transcribing the Egyptian writings the word or symbol representing 100 was mistaken for that representing 1,000. A similar mistake can occur today in English, where 'billion' means a thousand millions in an American text but a million millions in a British one, introducing a factor of error of a thousand millions.

According to J. F. Scott, 'the Egyptian system of counting was decimal, and the principle additive throughout. . . . The number 10 was denoted by a symbol like a capital U inverted; two such symbols stood for 20, and so on up to 90. A fresh sign, like coiled rope, was used for 100; another, a lotus flower, for 1,000.'

Professor Marinatos believes that the Egyptian priest 'unintentionally changed the centuries to millennia'. This would account for the date's mistake, but not for the mistakes in the dimensions of the plain in the Royal City. Others have explained the error in the numbers to that natural exaggeration which happens in all accounts handed down by tradition or word of mouth. And indeed, as any student of newspaper accounts of disasters must be aware, such exaggeration seems to be inevitable.

But in the Atlantis story there are two indications that the exaggeration of sizes is not due to tradition alone. If the numbers in the story had been increased by word of mouth the error in the dimensions of the plain of the Royal City and the error in the date of the submersion would hardly have been of precisely the same order of magnitude. Secondly, if Plato had heard the story from traditional sources, there would have been others who knew the tradition, and it is highly improbable that there should have been no mention of it in either Hesiod or Homer. The nature of the story can be found in Plato's own remarks.

The story was brought to Athens by Solon, who, on his return home, began writing about Atlantis on the basis of the notes he had made in Egypt; but was unable to complete his account because of the state of unrest he found in Athens on his return. After Solon's death the manuscripts relating to Atlantis came into the hands of Critias' grandfather and were eventually handed down to Critias himself. As Plato writes, Critias says: 'And these writings were in the possession of my grandfather and are actually now in mine, and when I was a child, I learnt them by heart' (*Crit.*, *113B*). And it is reasonable to suppose that Critias handed these writings to Plato, who was, after all, his nephew. Plato's account of Atlantis in the *Timaeus* is brief, only what he had heard from Critias; but it would seem that the story aroused great interest and Plato asked Critias for the notes. Plato then writes another dialogue, the *Critias*, in which he gives details of the Atlantis story, the dimensions of the Ancient Metropolis and the plan of the Royal City as well as the composition of the army. These details are so precise that they could have been preserved only in written records; and are, in any case, not the sort of interest to be preserved by word of mouth. The story of Atlantis breaks off in the *Critias*, but, as Plato has pointed out, Solon never had time or opportunity to finish it.

The story, then, is a detailed written account, brought from Egypt. Any errors or discrepancies in it are, so to speak, pre-Solon, and occur either in his transcription of the Egyptian records or in the Egyptian records themselves.

But how and why should the story of such a cataclysm have reached and survived in Egypt and not survived, except possibly vestigially, in Greece?

In the *Timaeus* (*25D*) Plato writes: 'The ocean at that spot has now become impassable and unsearchable, being blocked by the shoal mud which the island created as it settled down.' And this phenomenon is also mentioned in the *Critias*.

We have mentioned earlier the pumice ejected by the Coloumbos eruption in 1650. The floating layer locked up a sailing ship, was able to support large and small stones and even, reportedly, a man walking on it. After the eruption of Coseguina volcano in Nicaragua in 1835, according to Bullard 'the sea for 50 leagues was covered with floating masses of pumice resembling the floe-ice of the Northern Atlantic'. After the eruption of the Japanese volcano Sakurajima in January 1914 the ejecta floating on the sea were so thick that it was possible to walk on them to a distance of 23 miles. After the Krakatoa eruption of August 1883 the sea round the volcano was covered with pumice to a distance of 100 miles (160 km) and for many miles round the island this pumice was 13 ft (4 m) thick. The quantities of pumice hurled out by Stronghyle–Santorin in 1500 BC was certainly much greater—layers of pumice from this explosion have been found in Crete and Palestine; and the waves set up by the collapse of the centre of the volcano must have carried the floating pumice far and wide and the accumulation in coastal areas and shallows must have made navigation in the Aegean very difficult for some time.

The sound of the Krakatoa eruption was heard at a distance of 1,900 miles (3,000 km). The distance from Santorin to Alexandria is less than 450 miles (700 km) and the sound of the eruption of 1500 BC (three times greater than that of Krakatoa) must have been heard in Egypt with great intensity. The *tsunami* which followed the Chilean earthquake of May 1960 caused damage 10,700 miles (17,000 km) away. The *tsunami* which followed the collapse of Stronghyle–Santorin was at least half as powerful as the Chilean *tsunami*.

This brief review of volcanic phenomena is sufficient to show that the eruption and collapse of Stronghyle–Santorin must have had sensational effects of unusual violence, clearly perceptible in Egypt, which was at that time in close commercial contact with Minoan Crete. According to Professor Marinatos, the traffic between Crete and Egypt reached its high point at about the middle of the Second Millennium BC: 'The graves of Thebes depict the marvellous and rich products of the Minoan age that then flooded Egypt. The Egyptians must have imagined Crete as an immense and happy island, an "Atlantis".'

The effects of the *tsunamis* are particularly felt in those small bays which are especially suitable for harbours. The *tsunami* which followed the Japanese earthquake of AD 1707 sank more than 1,000 ships and boats in Osaka Bay. The giant *tsunami* of 1500 BC must have completely destroyed the merchant fleet and the warships of Crete. This unparalleled destruction must have struck the Minoan state a shattering blow and brought to a sudden end the traffic between Crete and Egypt. The catastrophe of 1500 BC certainly marked a stage in the development of Cretan and Aegean civilization.

In Crete, in particular, the human casualties, the destruction of property large and small and, above all, the annihilation of the shipping on which the prosperity and strength of Minoan Crete must very largely have depended, undoubtedly crippled the Minoans and gave to the aggressive Mycenaeans the chance to take over Crete and to assume the complete maritime and trading control of the east Mediterranean. The explosion of Santorin, at the very least, created a power vacuum in the Aegean—and made the way clear for the first Hellenization of Greece. It would have been very strange if events of such violence so strongly affecting the lives of the Eastern Mediterranean peoples, had not been recorded in detail by the culturally advanced people of Egypt.

At first sight it may seem strange that the disaster was not recorded by the Greeks and preserved only by the Egyptians. The answer appears in part in the *Timaeus* (*22B–23B*). Solon had been speaking to the Egyptians of the genealogies of the Greeks, when a very old Egyptian priest said:

' "Solon, you Greeks are always children: there is not such a thing as an old Greek" and on hearing this, he asked "What do you mean by this saying?" and the priest replied, "You are very young in soul, every one of you. For therein you possess not a single belief that is ancient and derived from old tradition, nor yet one science that is hoary with age. And this is the cause thereof: There have been and there will be many

PLATE 15. Excavations in progress at Akrotiri, with temporary buildings (right) covering the first house brought to light.

Minoan offering-bringers depicted in a tomb at Egyptian Thebes (from *The Palace of Minos* by Sir Arthur Evans).

and divers destructions of mankind, of which the greatest are by fire and water, and lesser ones by countless other means. For in truth the story that is told in your country as well as ours, how once upon a time Phaethon, son of Helios, yoked his father's chariot, and because he was unable to drive it along the course taken by his father, burnt up all that was upon the earth and himself perished by a thunderbolt—that story, as it is told, has the fashion of a legend, but the truth of it lies in the occurrence of a shifting of the bodies in the heavens which move round the earth, and a destruction of the things on the earth by fierce fire, which recur at long intervals. At such times all they that dwell on the mountains and in high and dry places suffer destruction more than those who dwell near to rivers or the sea; and in our case the Nile, our Saviour in other ways, saves us also at such times from this calamity by rising high. And when on the other hand, the Gods purge the earth with a flood of waters, all the herdsmen and shepherds that are in the mountains are saved, but those in the cities of your land are swept into the sea by the streams; whereas in our country neither then nor at any other time does the water pour down over our fields from above, on the contrary, it all tends naturally to well up from below. Hence it is, for these reasons, that what is here preserved is reckoned to be the most ancient; the truth being that in every place where there is no excessive heat or cold to prevent it, there always exists some human stock, now more, now less in number. And if any event has occurred that is noble or great or in any way conspicuous, whether it be in your country or in ours, or in some other place of which we know by report, all such events are recorded from of old and preserved here in our temples; whereas your people and the others are but newly equipped every time, with letters and all such arts as civilized states require: and when after the usual interval of years, the flood from heaven comes sweeping down afresh upon your people, it leaves none of you but the unlettered and uncultured, so that you become young as ever, with no knowledge of all that happened in old times in this land or in your own" . . . [and a little later, concerning the Athenian's ignorance of their own glorious past] "this has escaped your notice because for many generations the survivors died with no power to express themselves in writing."'

Likewise in the *Critias* (*109D–110A*): 'And of these citizens the names are preserved, but their works have vanished owing to the repeated destruction of their successors and the length of the intervening periods. For, as was said before, the stock that survived on each occasion, was a remnant of unlettered mountaineers which had heard the names only of the rulers, and but little besides of their works. . . . For legendary lore and the investigation of antiquity are visitants that come to cities in company with leisure, when they see that men are already furnished with the necessaries of life, and not before.'

In other words, Egypt, while aware of the cataclysm and perhaps suffering as a result of it (see Appendix B), was not overwhelmed by it,

PLATE 16. Painted *pithos* (storage jar) found in a domestic building excavated on Thera during the 1967 season.

whereas the islands and coasts of the Aegean suffered such terrible disaster that only their unlettered mountaineers survived, men unequipped for 'legendary lore and the investigation of antiquity' and concerned only with the basic necessity of survival. Yet, even so, later generations never forgot that Crete was rich and beautiful and great. Traditions and legends did survive and preserve hints and shadows of greatness and disaster—and the most striking of these is, of course, the story of Deucalion's Flood.

According to the most widely held tradition, Zeus wished to punish the descendants of the Titans for their wickedness and impiety and decided to destroy them in a flood. Prometheus, hearing of Zeus's intention, warned his son Deucalion. Deucalion, king of Phthia, built a boat for himself and his wife Pyrrha. In this they escaped when the waters covered Greece and drowned all its inhabitants; and their ship eventually came to rest on Mount Parnassus. They were then advised by an oracle to throw over their shoulders 'the bones of their mother'. Taking this (correctly) to refer to Mother Earth, they threw stones over their shoulders; and from the stones thrown by Deucalion sprang up men, from those thrown by Pyrrha, women. Their eldest son was Hellen, legendary ancestor of the Hellenic race and father of Dorus, Xuthus and Aeolus, the progenitors of respectively the Dorian, Ionian and Aeolian Greeks.

This legend is fully consonant with the Egyptian explanation and with the concept of disaster by water and the revival of life in the mountains.

Before considering more closely the analogies between central Crete and the Royal City of Atlantis, it is perhaps worthwhile to follow up yet again a reference in the Atlantis story to the physical conditions in Athens and to deduce from them the probable physical condition of central Crete.

In the *Critias* (*111E-112A*), it is said of Athens: 'In the first place, the Acropolis as it existed then, was different from what it is now. For as it is now, the action of a single night of extraordinary rain has crumbled it away and made it bare of soil, when earthquakes occurred simultaneously with the third of the disastrous floods which preceded the destructive deluge in the time of Deucalion. But in its former extent, at an earlier period, it went down towards the Eridanus and the Ilissus and embraced within it the Pnyx, and had Lycabettus as its boundary over against the Pnyx; and it was all rich in soil and, save for a small space, level on top.'

Torrential rain is a volcanic phenomenon. During eruptions the steam and other gases issuing from the crater reach great heights, are condensed, and fall in the form of rain. During the Vesuvius eruption of 1872 ash and gases reached a height of 5 miles (8 km) and after condensation produced a deluge of rain and mud over a large area. In the famous eruption of Vesuvius in AD 79 the town of Herculaneum was covered with a stream of mud—water mixed with volcanic ash. The energy released by this famous eruption was, however, only about one-thousandth of that released by the Krakatoa eruption of 1883—or something in the nature of one-three-thousandth of the eruption of Stronghyle-Santorin.

But volcanic eruptions can cause heavy rainfall in another way. The small particles of volcanic ash rise to a great height and may become nuclei for the condensation of water vapour and so start precipitation. Heavy rainfalls, therefore, even in such notoriously dry areas as Attica, can be easily accounted for as a volcanic phenomenon, such as might be expected before the final cataclysm.

If, as Plato records, the morphology of Athens was so drastically changed by rainfall, it would seem that the central basin of Crete must have been changed to, at least, a similar degree. The surface layer of this basin is neogene, consisting of comparatively recent rocks which are less consolidated and so subject to fast erosion. About 3,500 years ago the central basin of Crete must have been much richer in soil than it is now and also, except for a few hills, practically level.

Assuming, then, that Crete would meet the geographical requirements of Atlantis, would the Minoan civilization match in any way that of Atlantis? The parallels are strong and striking.

The eruption of Vesuvius in 1872, showing the huge clouds of gas and ash thrown out by the volcano.

The decipherment of the Linear-B tablets found at Knossos has shown that around 1400 BC the language spoken there was an early form of Greek; and, as shown by John Chadwick, among the four names of gods found in the tablets one is Poseidon in its Homeric form *Poseidaon*. According to Chadwick the Greeks (by whom are meant people speaking a language recognizable as Greek) invaded Greece about 2100 BC, spreading out from around Argos and conquering Knossos in the fifteenth century BC. These are the people we usually speak of as Mycenaeans. Athens, it should be remembered, was a Mycenaean city at this period. On the Acropolis today, in deep levels near the Parthenon, Mycenaean walling can still be seen. History, chronology and tradition all support the notion of a confrontation of Mycenaean/Athenians with Minoan/ Atlanteans. Theseus, the Athenian hero who killed the Minotaur and freed Athens from the dominion of Minos, was a Mycenaean.

But the earliest inhabitants of Crete, who appear there in the Fourth Millennium BC, are of course pre-Greek and, whatever their origins, the Minoans must have reached Crete via the Cyclades; and indeed Cycladic influence is quite evident in early Minoan Crete. Before reaching Crete they must have settled in the fertile islands of Santorin and Melos. And the settlement of the Minoans in Santorin may be equated with the arrival of Poseidon to wed Cleito, daughter of Evenor and Leucippe and so to found the Atlantean dynasty. These Early Minoan settlers would find a Santorin rich in springs and with a rich vegetation of *Phoenix dactylifera*, *Chamaerops humilis*, *Pistacia lentiscus* and the olive (*Olea europaea*). Its fertility may be presumed from its earliest historical name, Pindar, Callimachus, Apollonius Rhodius, Pliny and Pausanias all mentioning that the original name of Thera was Kalliste (the most beautiful).

The crossing from Santorin to Crete must have called for courage and enterprise in the peoples of the Early Cycladic period (2800–2000 BC). For this, they would have needed ships with keels; and in fact the people of the Cyclades were the first to use keeled ships in the Eastern Mediterranean. The voyage of the Argonauts under Jason from Greece, through the Dardanelles and the Bosphorus, to the far coasts of the Black Sea is, of course, a legend; but legends are usually based on fact. And in the extraordinary Treasure of Dorak, found in royal tombs on the south shore of the Sea of Marmara and dating from around 2500 BC, was found a sword, its blade engraved with several sea-going ships, equipped with sails

Linear B tablet from Crete bearing the name of Poseidon in its Homeric form *Poseidaon*, evidence of Greek influence in Knossos.

Mycenaean walling below the Parthenon on the Acropolis at Athens, which was a Mycenaean city at the time of the Atlantis disaster.

and banks of oars. Crete had fertile plains and mountains covered with extensive forests of oak, cypress and pine; and taking advantage of this abundance, its inhabitants soon established large shipyards and built the largest navy and mercantile fleet in the Mediterranean. The many port facilities and appliances discovered in the island are proof of this and the fame of the Cretan fleets has been celebrated in those traditions which lay stress on the Cretan thalassocracy (mastery of the seas). It is generally supposed that from 2400 BC until the fall of Knossos all the trade of the Eastern Mediterranean was in the hands of Minoan Crete. According to Diodorus, Crete 'lay very favourably for voyages all over the world', and by 'world' Diodorus would mean the Greek world of the Eastern Mediterranean.

With this powerful navy the Cretans reached the nearest shores of Africa and established their first colonies in Cyrenaica; and indeed in Early Minoan Crete the African influence is derived, according to Professor Marinatos, more from Libya than from Egypt. During the Middle Minoan period there was close contact with Africa and between 2100 and 1500 BC there was continuous traffic between Crete and Egypt, with reciprocal influence in both countries.

Like Atlantis, Crete was densely populated, especially during the

Middle Minoan period, a fact of which its 90–100 towns are proof. Rich from trade and war, the Cretans built the famous palaces at Phaistos and Knossos (plate 19), the latter, the capital city of Minos, being the 'Great City' of Homer. Towards the end of the Middle Minoan period, some years before the eruption and submergence of central Santorin, civilization in Crete and the Aegean reached its height, with the Minoan state at the pinnacle of its power and glory. In that period (1580–1500 BC) Aegeus, the mythical king of Athens and father of Theseus, was defeated by Minos and Athens became a state tributary to Crete. According to the myth, Theseus later went to Crete and freed the Athenians from the tribute Minos had forced them to pay. Minos, ruler of Minoan Crete, is considered as the founder of Cretan sea power and the builder of many towns on the island. The liberation of Athens from the domination of Minoan Crete and the victory of the Athenians over the islanders of Atlantis are evidently traditions referring to the same historical event.

Minoan Crete was early concerned in metal working and metal trading. First copper and bronze were used, especially in the manufacture of knives and other tools and weapons. Traditionally Crete was the first great metal-working centre of Europe; and yet, relatively speaking, metal artefacts of Minoan Crete are not outstandingly numerous. Bronze objects, tools including long saws, daggers, knives and swords, have indeed been found, and quantities of small gold jewellery; but compared with Mycenaean sites, the quantities are small. The famous gold cups are usually from mainland and Mycenaean sites though very probably made

Sword blade from the Dora treasure depicting a variety seagoing ships of Cycladic type. Such ships may have carried settlers from Santorin to Crete.

Reconstruction drawings of the Queen's Megaron and the Hall of the Double Axe in the palace of Knossos (from Evans: *Palace of Minos*).

Two seagoing ships of Crete, depicted on seal-stones (from Evans: *Palace of Minos*).

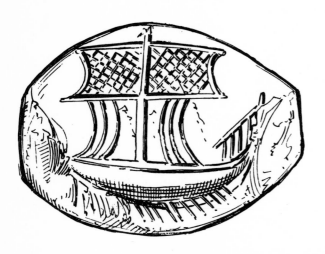

142

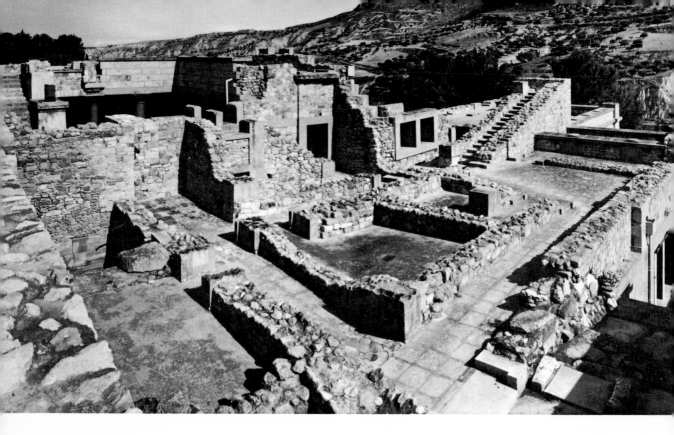

Part of the ruins of the palace of Knossos, the 'Great City' of Homer.

by Minoan craftsmen, and there is nothing in Crete comparable with the gold masks of Mycenae which led Schliemann to observe that he had looked upon the face of Agamemnon. But compared with the warrior aristocracy of the Mycenaeans with their tendency to male display, the Minoan world seems like a rich and sophisticated bourgeoisie in which men and women are much more equal, and women enjoy the fruits of luxury and frivolity, with fanciful clothes, elaborate coiffures and elegant rather than splendid jewellery. The Minoans, too, suffered an absorption

The elaborate clothes and hairstyles of the Minoan women are depicted in these two frescoes from Knossos (*left* and *top right*) and in the gold seal (*right*) from a Minoan royal tomb at Isopata, near Knossos.

144

by the Mycenaeans; ancient metals, especially bronze and gold, are valuable and can be melted into multiple re-use. The gold of the conquered melts without trace into the gold of the conquerors. True, the Mycenaeans, too, ended in disaster, but, if we are to believe the credible theories of such scholars as Professor Rhys Carpenter, their disaster was drought and famine; and their successors in the Peloponnese, the Dorians, entered an empty land in which the treasures lay in forgotten tombs.

Even so, it is quite clear that the Minoans, like Plato's Atlanteans, were familiar with metals, skilled in their use and exploitation and, most probably, carrying on a sea-borne trade in ores, ingots and finished metal products. Minoan influence in Cyprus, the principal ancient source of copper, is evident about 1500 BC. Tin was most probably imported from Dorylaeon (Eskisehir) in Asia Minor, the trade with Tartessos in Spain and with Cornwall and the Cassiterides (whether these are identified with the Scillies or with islands at the mouth of the Loire) being somewhat later in date.

The agricultures of Atlantis and Crete have much in common. It is mentioned that the inhabitants of Atlantis irrigated their land, using rainwater in winter and water from the springs in summer. This fact shows that there was little or no rainfall in summer and that the climate of Atlantis was Mediterranean in type. In Atlantis, wheat, vines and especially olives grew on the plains. The olive is a xerophytic (or dry climate) tree, characteristic of the Mediterranean basin and growing in a subtropical climate between Lat. 32° and 45° in both hemispheres.

P. Anagnostopoulos, who has studied the origin of the olive, has concluded that the cultivation of the olive began in Crete before the Third Millennium BC; and that from Crete it was taken about 2000 BC to Egypt (where it did not thrive) and at about 1800 BC to the islands of the Aegean, Asia Minor, Palestine and mainland Greece. From Greece, its cultivation was spread by Greek colonists to Italy, Sicily, southern France, Spain and the West.

The Minoan polity had much in common with that of Atlantis. Minoan Crete was densely populated; so, in Plato's account, was Atlantis. Atlantis was divided into villages and settlements each with a leader and a uniform organization and all subject to the Royal City. The great numbers of luxurious buildings of Minoan Crete clearly indicates that there were provincial governors at distances of 6–12 miles (10–20 km) apart, governing in the King's name. The King appears to have been the supreme political and religious leader and, in accordance with the hierocratic nature of the Minoan regime, the provincial governor would be a lesser king dependent on the priest–king, a sort of combined prefect and bishop.

The bull is a principal and well-known feature of Minoan art and life. The legendary Minotaur (which Theseus slew) was half-bull, half-man; splendid rhytons were made in the form of bull's heads; the pursuit of the bull is a favourite sport and subject of art; and, best known of all, there

Excavated remains of villas at Tylissos, in northern Crete, some six miles west of Knossos.

'The bull is a principal and well-known feature of Minoan art and life.' *Right* Terracotta rhyton in the form of a bull with tiny human figures clinging to its horns and muzzle, from a tomb at Koumasa in the Messara plain. *Overleaf* Rhyton in the shape of a bull's head, made of steatite, found at Kato Zakro in eastern Crete. *Overleaf, facing page* The famous bull-leap fresco from Knossos (*upper picture*), which is echoed in the mural of a bull and hunters (*below*) found at Çatal Hüyük in Anatolia.

146

were the bull-leaping games in which young men and girls performed incredibly acrobatic and dangerous feats in the bull-ring. These last find an early echo in the murals recently found at Çatal Hüyük in Anatolia, which show men similarly engaged in teasing bulls and other major and dangerous animals. These incidentally, date from about 5850 BC and give support to the notion that the early Cretans came, via the Cyclades, from Central Anatolia.

The bull was likewise a cult animal in Atlantis, as appears in a passage in the *Critias* (*119C–120D*), which is important in this and several other respects. It reads:

'Each of the kings ruled over the men and most of the land in his own particular portion and throughout his own city, punishing and putting to death whomsoever he willed. But their authority over one another and their mutual relations were governed by the precepts of Poseidon, as handed down to them by the law and by the records inscribed by the first princes on a pillar of orichalcum, which was placed within the Temple of Poseidon in the centre of the island; and thither they assembled every fifth year, and then alternately every sixth year—giving equal honour to both the even and odd—and when thus assembled they took counsel about public affairs and inquired if they had in any way transgressed and gave judgement. And when they were about to give judgement they first gave pledges to one another of the following descriptions. In the sacred precincts of Poseidon there were bulls at large; and the ten princes being alone by themselves, after praying to the God that they might capture a victim well-pleasing unto him, hunted after the bulls with staves and nooses, but with no weapons of iron; and whatever bull they captured they led up to the pillar and cuts its throat over the top of the pillar, raining down blood on the inscription. And inscribed upon the pillar, besides the laws, was an oath which involved mighty curses upon them that disobeyed. When, then, they had done sacrifice according to their laws, and were consecrating all the limbs of the bull, they mixed a bowl of wine and poured in on behalf of each one a gout of blood, and the rest they carried to the fire, when they had first purged the pillars round about. And after this they drew from the bowl with golden ladles, and making libation at the fire swore to give judgement according to the laws upon the pillar and to punish whosoever had committed any previous transgression; and, moreover, that henceforth they would not transgress any of the writing willingly, nor govern nor submit to any governor's edict save in accordance with their father's laws. And when each of them had made this invocation both for himself and for his seed after him, he drank of the cup and offered it up as a gift in the temple of the God; and after spending the interval in supping and necessary business, when darkness came on and the sacrificial fire had died down, all the princes robed themselves in most beautiful sable vestments and sat on the ground beside the cinders of the sacramental victims throughout the night, extinguishing all

The capture of a netted bull, depicted in one of the gold cups from Vaphio, provides an interesting reminder of Plato's description of the nobles of Atlantis hunting bulls 'with staves and nooses, but with no weapons of iron'.

the fire that was round about the sanctuary; and there they gave and received judgement, they wrote the judgements, when it was light, upon a golden tablet, and dedicated them together with their robes as memorials. And there were many other special laws concerning the peculiar rights of the several princes, whereof the most important were these: that they should never take up arms against one another, and that should anyone attempt to overthrow in any city their royal house, they should all lend aid, taking counsel in common, like their forerunners, concerning their policy in war and other matters, while conceding the leadership to the royal branch of Atlas; and that the King had no authority to put to death any of his brother-princes save with the consent of more than half the ten.'

Two points emerge here which are interesting though subsidiary to the total picture. The first is the reference to the meetings of the kings on, alternately, every fifth and sixth year. Plato says that this was because

they wished to honour alike the odd and even numbers. This is not an entirely convincing explanation, as the first and second years or third and fourth would be equally valid. The choice of fifth and sixth could possibly mean that the Kings of Atlantis were aware of the eleven-year cycle of rains and assembled at the times of maximum and minimum activity of sun-spots. According to B. Eginitis, the eleven-year cycle of rains, which Theophrastus (371–257 BC) mentions as known in antiquity, was known in pre-Homeric times and specifically in Minoan times as 'nine year' (*enneateris* or *enneoros*) and quotes the *Odyssey* in support: 'Among their cities is the great city Knossos, where Minos reigned through periods of nine years, he that held converse with great Zeus.' And Plato in the *Laws* (*624B*) interprets these lines as meaning that Minos went every nine years to the cave on Mount Ida where he met Zeus who handed him the laws. Minos, like the Kings of Atlantis, is shown as presenting and administering laws of divine origin.

The second point concerns 'the most beautiful sable vestments' which

Fresco from Amnisos that has been thought to symbolize 'the Kingdom of the two islands'— Crete and Santorin.

the princes assume in the second stage of the ceremonies. The word translated in this version as 'sable' is *kuanos*, which is more usually taken to mean 'blue', and as J. G. Bennett has pointed out: 'The frescoes of Knossos show that blue was the royal colour, and there is evidence that the blue dye first reached Asia from the Cretan traders.'

A possible link between Crete and Atlantis lies in one of the frescoes which was found in the villa at Amnisos, the port of Knossos. This shows a symbol which signifies 'sea' in a double form, the smaller example resting immediately above the larger example. Professor Marinatos has put forward the interesting interpretation that this indicates 'the Kingdom of the two islands, the major and the minor'; and this reading could fit equally Crete and Santorin, or the Ancient Metropolis and Royal City of Atlantis.

A curious and vivid light on the Minoan life of Santorin before the eruption was thrown by the discovery in 1966 by Mr Edward Loring of a fossilized monkey's head. It has been examined by Professor C. Eliakis, a specialist in post-mortem examination, who finds that it shows a multiple fracture caused by a blunt heavy object—probably a hot volcanic bomb which rapidly cooled. The excellent preservation of the features is thought to be due to the high temperature; and, according to Dr Paraskevopoulos, Professor of Mineralogy and Petrology, after this embalming by heat, the organic matter of the head was replaced by andesite lava of the same texture as that found in Santorin. Dr A. Poulianos, Professor of Anthropology, identifies it as a gibbon, probably of the species *Colobinae*, mostly found in Ethiopia. The fossil was found near Monolithos, on the east coast of Thera, and it may be that it was thrown there, already fossilized, in a parasitic eruption later in date than that which caused the animal's death.

Its presence in pre-eruption Santorin is, of course, the interesting factor. It is not a native animal and it has no economic purpose. It must therefore have been a pet, imported from Africa, presumably through the Egyptian trade. The keeping of imported pets does after all imply a certain standard of prosperity and luxury, to say nothing of wide external contacts; and it has, in fact, always been assumed that the Minoans did keep monkeys as pets in view of such representations as the Fresco of the Blue Monkey picking papyrus flowers and that of the Saffron Gatherer, which is now usually interpreted to show a monkey rather than a man. Even so, such rare imported animals would most likely be pets of the palace rather than of the common people; and the presence of one in Santorin does strengthen the island's claim to have been in an especial relationship with Minoan Crete, to have been, in fact, the Ancient Metropolis to the Royal City.

But interesting though these Minoan–Atlantean parallels are, it is the general picture which is the more impressive, the internal unity and ordered peace of the inhabitants of Atlantis evoking so strongly that *Pax Minoica* under which, according to Marinatos, the mild, idyllic and peaceful civilization of the united states of Minoan Crete developed.

Overleaf Fossilized monkey's head found on Santorin in 1966. *Overleaf, facing page* The Blue Monkey fresco from Knossos (*upper picture*) and the Saffron Gatherer fresco from Knossos, which is now thought to depict a monkey. Monkeys were not native to Crete, but were imported from Africa, probably as pets. The presence of a pet monkey on Santorin is further evidence of the island's relationship with Minoan Crete.

Rhyton from Pseira decorated with dolphins, a frequent motif in Minoan art.

An ivory seal of the Early Minoan period in Crete, in the form of a monkey.

Admittedly such general impressions tend to be atmospheric and subjective, but subjective impressions arise out of innumerable objective facts and congruences. Once the parallelism of Atlantis and Minoan Crete is considered, numbers of details fall into place. Among the animals described as living in Atlantis is the elephant. The pigmy elephant certainly lived in Crete, before the melting of the ice-sheets, as it did likewise in Malta; and, although it is unlikely to have survived into Bronze Age times, the skulls may well have been known, and it is an odd fact that many ivory seals of early Minoan times have been found whereas in Middle Minoan times, when traffic with Egypt was much greater, ivory seals were no longer made. The descriptions of the interior of the Temple of Poseidon in Atlantis includes mention of nereids sitting on dolphins; and dolphins were a favourite motif of Minoan art.

Moreover the links between Minoan Crete and Stronghyle–Santorin are increasingly apparent. In the past, pottery of Minoan influence and manufacture of about 1550 BC has been found in the island together with a sword bearing gold axe symbols. Such discoveries, dating from 1867, gave the impression that there was at least a Minoan outpost on the island —which, is, after all, the nearest of the Cyclades to Crete. On the island of Melos, only a little more distant from Crete, Phylacopi is described by Professor Marinatos as being completely under Minoan influence and possibly an actual Minoan colony. The import of obsidian from Melos to Crete had begun as early as 3000 BC. Obsidian is that black volcanic glass

Nineteenth-century finds on Santorin provide interesting comparisons with Minoan objects from Crete. An alabaster beaker from Thera (*below left*) closely resembles two beakers found recently at Kato Zakro. The right-hand beaker is made of obsidian, which was imported to Crete from Melos from a very early period.

The decoration of lilies on a vase from Knossos, of the Middle Minoan period (*left*) closely resembles that on a jug from Thera (*above right*). *Right* Sword blade found on Thera in 1867, decorated with gold axes, and a similar sword blade from a tomb at Pylos, in the Peloponnese; the resemblance suggests a close association between Santorin and mainland Greece.

which flakes to give a razor-sharp edge and was highly prized in Neolithic times by all those peoples who had access to it, as it made edged-tools superior even to those of flint. The island of Melos was the great Aegean source of this valuable material and wherever in the area obsidian tools are found it is assumed that the inhabitants were in trading contact with Melos. It is therefore hardly surprising that such dominant sea-traders as the Minoans should have been in close relations with this island and its highly prized raw material.

But in 1967 excavations at Akrotiri in the southernmost part of Thera (plates 13, 14, 15) put the close link between Minoan Crete and Stronghyle–Santorin beyond any doubt. These excavations were directed

Two marble harpists from Thera, dating from the end of the second millennium BC.

by Professor Spyridon Marinatos for the Archaeological Society of Athens with the collaboration of Mrs Emily Vermeule, Boston Museum of Fine Arts, and Mr James W. Mavor of the Woods Hole Oceanographic Institute. The results of this excavation are known to be of a revolutionary nature although still only at the exploratory stage. What they have revealed seems to be a Bronze Age 'Pompeii'. Nine trenches were sunk and some thirty-five donkey-loads of artefacts were taken to the museum in Phera for further study; and it is clear that a considerable township lies buried, virtually intact, under massive layers of volcanic ash and pumice. At one point there is a tall exposed face of this *pozzolana*. A trial hole, some 10–15 ft deep, reveals, below all this volcanic overburden, a stretch of stone walling. Nearby a domestic building was uncovered containing still standing and intact Late Minoan I painted storage vessels, and wooden fragments of a loom with scattered loom weights (plates 16, 17). A little further away the spade has already uncovered a façade of those large ashlar blocks which in a Minoan context indicate a palace or nobleman's villa. Elsewhere shattered fragments of painted plaster appear.

Still more fragments of fresco appeared when the excavations were renewed in 1968. On most of them plant and bird designs appeared. On one there is an animal form which is probably that of a blue monkey, especially interesting in relation to the fossilized monkey's head found a few years ago; another shows a drooping palm tree and the head of a thick-lipped young man, possibly significant of the link with Libya. The buildings previously located under about 10 feet of pumice were further explored by means of a tunnel following a paved way. This might prove to be a street or part of a courtyard, but the tunnel at this time was too narrow to provide full evidence. The building revealed had window openings in which there were traces of wooden frames and had been two

Recent excavations on Thera by Professor Spyridon Marinatos have strengthened the links between Santorin and the civilization of Minoan Crete. The photograph shows an early stage of the excavation, in the summer of 1967.

storeys high, although the upper storey had collapsed. A good deal of this season was devoted to making a canal to divert possible winter torrents which might cause the workings to collapse. This labour was justified by Professor Marinatos's belief that this was indeed the main settlement of Minoan Thera, and that major finds were likely to be made in the future.

So far no skeletons and no precious objects have been found—in fact to the uninstructed eye all that appears is a number of fragmentary stone walls deep in a landscape of volcanic dust, traversed by even dustier paths, dominated by the small village of Akrotiri with its ruined Venetian castle, illuminated with the brilliant sun and the not far distant deep blue sea, among fields of the almost prostrate Santorini vines; but the implications are tremendous. The visitor is standing above the buried but intact ruins of a considerable Minoan township of the most sophisticated period, overwhelmed with the world's most stupendous outpouring of pumice and volcanic ash some 3,500 years ago. This was a terrific disaster, remorseless and on a gigantic scale but possibly gradual; now it begins to look as if the inhabitants had time to flee, snatching up their valuables and, perhaps, making their escape by sea. What would be their fate then, it is hard to say. Some may have reached the neighbouring islands of Ios and Anaphi, some the more distant shores of Melos and

Professor Marinatos directing digging operations on Thera, 1967.

Some of the pottery found during recent excavations on Thera. The shapes and decoration bear a close resemblance to those of Minoan pottery from Crete. The three pots just below the centre of the photograph show cracks that are probably due to the intense heat of the volcanic eruption that destroyed the settlement.

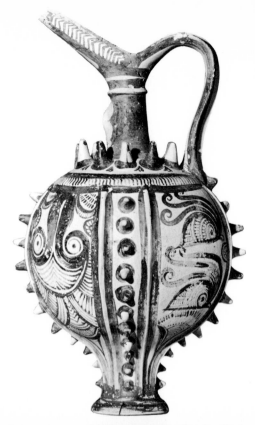

Crete. Even so, bearing in mind the colossal outpouring of ash and pumice, they may have found there descending blankets of death only a little less obliterating than those which fell on Santorin. But even more probable is it that like the ship locked in the floating pumice by the Coloumbos eruption of 1650, their frail and open boats, crowded with human beings and their treasured possessions, were sooner or later immobilized in the floating pumice, buried in the endlessly falling ash, until death by drowning or suffocation ended their miseries. Additional horror lies in the fact that this falling ash may have been extremely hot. In 1956, some human teeth were found in a *pozzolana* mine near Phera, some belonging to a man of between 30–35, others to a woman of 40–45. Two of these teeth were charred—which implies that the temperature of the volcanic ash was very high even after falling. But whatever their fate— and some, like the Ancient Mariner, may have survived—their homes and their country were totally and irretrievably covered in ash, their civilization completely disrupted. And this volcanic action, by emptying the magma chamber beneath the island, also led, after a period of years not yet clearly defined or even definable, to that colossal and unparalleled collapse of the centre of the island which set up the gigantic waves which wrecked an Aegean civilization.

The case for identifying the Stronghyle–Santorin disaster with the submersion of Atlantis is, in total, immensely strong; for identifying it with the Ancient Metropolis, most impressive; and, since Santorin is now conclusively shown to have been Minoan and since the Minoan Empire suffered a catastrophic disaster at the time of the collapse of Santorin, the case for identifying Atlantis with Minoan Crete seems so strong as to be unanswerable.

Atlantis and Minoan Crete then merge together into a single picture— a rich and powerful state, theoretically an ancient theocracy under a priest-king, in actuality a prosperous *haute bourgeoisie*, frivolous and sophisticated, delighting in strange spectacles and daring sports, wearing clothes of fashionable elegance, using pottery of great beauty and excessive fantasy, enjoying, apparently, a freedom and equality of the sexes unusual in antiquity, a civilization entrancing, decadent, delightful— and doomed.

'Pottery of great beauty and excessive fantasy' exemplifies the delightful civilization of Minoan Crete—and of Atlantis.

EPILOGUE

Epilogue

From time to time in the history of human intelligence, men, and learned men at that, have delighted to tease themselves with insoluble riddles— from 'what song the Sirens sang' to the number of angels who could dance upon a needle, from the grand elixir for transmuting base metals to gold to the secret of perpetual youth, from the pyramids of Egypt and the lost tribes of Israel to the Atlantis of Plato.

In all these fields the learned enthusiast and the scientific amateur are commonly found. For them the search is all, the overtones, the implications, the whole cosmology which develops around these enquiries are so vast (and often so cloudy) that the solution would be an anticlimax, even a sort of bathos. For them the journey is all, the destination so impossible, almost by definition, of achievement; for them it is far better hopefully to travel than actually to arrive. Egyptologists despair when confronted with the calculations of pyramidomaniacs, as they call them; the very word 'Atlantis' casts a chill over the rational man.

For in the more than 2,300 years since Plato the innumerable attempts to solve the riddle of Atlantis have increased the mystery rather than solved it. The fact, Atlantis, has become for them the metaphysical concept, Atlantis.

Enthusiastic imagination has endowed the islanders with exceptional bodily, intellectual and political powers. They are the zenith from which we have declined to our present nadir. Many modern discoveries, most of our modern scientific knowledge, are credited to them. Atlantis is the land, they know, from which all modern civilization descends. Atlantis was the Golden Age. Atlantis, with the burden of all their theories, has become more legendary than its supposedly myth-like appearance in the pages of Plato. In the hands of such enthusiasts, Atlantis ceases to be Plato's Atlantis, it becomes to the enthusiast 'my Atlantis' and embodies 'my theories', 'my ideology', 'my dreams' and, possibly to satisfy 'my patriotism', is located in odder and odder and more surprising corners of the globe.

In such a climate, a simple and logical solution is unwelcome. In such conditions of particular enthusiasm and general incredulity, any evidence, however convincing, on the actual history and real geographical location of Atlantis, is greeted with scepticism. To persuade a large number of persons, either biased or indifferent, is a venture of very doubtful success;

man is by nature attracted to the mysterious and the removal of the mystery—especially when the solution is simple—is more likely to produce disappointment than satisfaction.

Nevertheless the conviction of the correctness of the solution—reached in an indirect fashion through studies of *tsunamis* observed on the Greek shores since antiquity—led to the decision of one of the authors (A. G. G.) to present it formally on 1 August 1960 at a special symposium on seismic sea-waves and Aeolian waves held by the Associations of Seismology and Physics of the Earth's Interior, Meteorology and Oceanography at the Helsinki XIIth General Assembly of the International Union of Geodesy and Geophysics. The favourable reception given to it by a large number of fellow-members and the echo that followed in the world's press were enough to encourage a wider investigation of the subject. The outcome of this wider research was the announcement to the Athens Academy four months later of a complete and integrated solution of the Atlantis riddle.

The solution of this riddle is as simple as the mistake which created it. The Atlantis story in Plato is essentially correct in all its points except the date of the submersion of the Ancient Metropolis which was 900 years and not 9,000 years before Solon, and the dimensions of the plain of the Royal City, which should be 300 × 200 stades and not 3,000 × 2,000, as given in Plato. It may be reasonably deduced that this erroneous factor of 10 crept in during the transcriptions of the Egyptian records. The Ancient Metropolis was the island of Santorin before the submergence of its central part and the plain of the Royal City was the central basin of Crete. The dominion of Minoan Crete extended from Libya to the frontiers of Egypt and in Europe as far as Tyrrhenia. By the standards of the city-states of antiquity, the Minoan state was indeed immense.

At the height of its power a prodigious volcanic eruption brought about the collapse of the central and presumably holiest and most significant part of the Ancient Metropolis and buried the remainder under layers of volcanic ash and pumice. Concurrently with this collapse, which presumably took place some years, even tens of years, after the deposition of the pumice which obliterated the Ancient Metropolis, *tsunamis*, gravity sea waves of a height unparalleled in history, devastated the shores of the Eastern Mediterranean, laying waste the cities of Minoan Crete and destroying the greatest fleet of the time. In that collapse of the central part of the island, the heart of the Ancient Metropolis, its central temple and inner harbours, already covered with thick pumice, disappeared beneath the waves in destructive temperatures of the magnitude of 1,350 °C.

This suggested solution is not based on conjecture or myths but on a geological occurrence beyond challenge. It may be expressed perhaps in this fashion. In the high Bronze Age around 1500 BC a dominant maritime power, Atlantis, threatening both Egypt and Athens, disappeared in a single day and night in a frightful natural cataclysm. Around 1500 BC a round island in the Aegean with now-known Minoan connections—

Stronghyle–Santorin—collapsed into the sea in a large volcanic eruption with side effects which caused such devastation to Minoan Crete—a dominant sea-power in contact with both Athens and Egypt—that this Minoan Empire never recovered. Is it conceivable that two such unprecedented disasters happened at the same time, in the same area, in the same circumstances? Is it not clear that they are one and the same disaster? In fact, can it be doubted that the Ancient Metropolis and Royal City of Atlantis were Stronghyle–Santorin and Minoan Crete?

There are many who contend that the Atlantean culture was the origin of civilization. We do not know if the same has been claimed for the Creto–Minoan culture. It is, however, generally accepted that classical Greek culture, the principal source of Western civilization, had its roots in Mycenaean Greece and Minoan Crete.

APPENDICES

Appendix A

This appendix consists of the following extracts: *Timaeus 20D–26E*, pp. 28–47, *Critias 108D–121C*, pp. 267–307.[1]

TIMAEUS

20   CRIT. Listen then, Socrates, to a tale which, though passing
E strange, is yet wholly true, as Solon, the wisest of the Seven, once
upon a time declared. Now Solon—as indeed he often says himself in his poems—was a relative and very dear friend of our great-
grandfather Dropides; and Dropides told our grandfather Critias
—as the old man himself, in turn, related to us—that the exploits
of this city in olden days, the record of which had perished through
time and the destruction of its inhabitants, were great and
marvellous, the greatest of all being one which it would be proper
21 for us now to relate both as a payment of our debt of thanks to
you and also as a tribute of praise, chanted as it were duly and
truly, in honour of the Goddess on this her day of Festival.

     SOC. Excellent! But come now, what was this exploit described
by Critias, following Solon's report, as a thing not verbally
recorded, although actually performed by this city long ago?

     CRIT. I will tell you: it is an old tale, and I heard it from a man
not young. For indeed at that time, as he said himself, Critias was
B already close upon ninety years of age, while I was somewhere
about ten; and it chanced to be that day of the Apaturia which is
called 'Cureotis'. The ceremony for boys which was always
customary at the feast was held also on that occasion, our fathers
arranging contests in recitation. So while many poems of many
poets were declaimed, since the poems of Solon were at that time
new, many of us children chanted them. And one of our fellow-
tribesmen—whether he really thought so at the time or whether
C he was paying a compliment to Critias—declared that in his
opinion Solon was not only the wisest of men in all else, but in
poetry also he was of all poets the noblest. Whereat the old man
(I remember the scene well) was highly pleased and said with a
smile, 'If only, Amynander, he had not taken up poetry as a by-

---

[1]Reprinted by permission of the publishers and the Loeb Classical Library from Plato's *Timaeus, Critias, Cleitophon, Menexenus, Epistles* (trans. R. G. Bury), Harvard University Press, Cambridge, Mass.: William Heinemann Ltd, London.

play but had worked hard at it like others, and if he had completed the story he brought here from Egypt, instead of being
D forced to lay it aside owing to the seditions and all the other evils
he found here on his return—why then, I say, neither Hesiod nor
Homer nor any other poet would ever have proved more famous
than he.' 'And what was the story, Critias?' said the other. 'Its
subject,' replied Critias, 'was a very great exploit, worthy indeed
to be accounted the most notable of all exploits, which was performed by this city, although the record of it has not endured until
now owing to lapse of time and the destruction of those who
wrought it.' 'Tell us from the beginning,' said Amynander, 'what
Solon related and how, and who were the informants who
vouched for its truth.'

E   'In the Delta of Egypt,' said Critias, 'where, at its head, the
stream of the Nile parts in two, there is a certain district called the
Saitic. The chief city in this district is Sais—the home of King
Amasis—the founder of which, they say, is a goddess whose
Egyptian name is Neïth, and in Greek, as they assert, Athena.
These people profess to be great lovers of Athens and in a measure
akin to our people here. And Solon said that when he travelled
there he was held in great esteem amongst them; moreover, when
he was questioning such of their priests as were most versed in
ancient lore about their early history, he discovered that neither
he himself nor any other Greek knew anything at all, one might
say, about such matters. And on one occasion, when he wished to
draw them on to discourse on ancient history, he attempted to tell
them the most ancient of our traditions, concerning Phoroneus,
who was said to be the first man, and Niobe; and he went on to
tell the legend about Deucalion and Pyrrha after the Flood, and
B how they survived it, and to give the genealogy of their descendants; and by recounting the number of years occupied by the
events mentioned he tried to calculate the periods of time. Where-
upon one of the priests, a prodigiously old man, said, 'O Solon,
Solon, you Greeks are always children: there is not such a thing
as an old Greek.' And on hearing this he asked, 'What mean you
by this saying?' And the priest replied, 'You are young in soul,
every one of you. For therein you possess not a single belief that is
ancient and derived from old tradition, nor yet one science that is
C hoary with age. And this is the cause thereof: There have been
and there will be many and divers destructions of mankind, of
which the greatest are by fire and water, and lesser ones by countless other means. For in truth the story that is told in your country
as well as ours, how once upon a time Phaethon, son of Helios,
yoked his father's chariot, and, because he was unable to drive it
along the course taken by his father, burnt up all that was upon
the earth and himself perished by a thunderbolt—that story, as

22

PLATE 17. In the same
building on Thera as the
pithos in Plate 16, were found
wooden fragments of a loom
and scattered loom weights.

Overleaf PLATE 18. Part of the
Messara plain, in south-
central Crete, with the Ida
Mountains in the distance. The
Messara plain matches Plato's
description of the plain of the
Royal City of Atlantis.

Overleaf, facing page PLATE 19.
An aerial view of part of the
palace of Knossos, in northern
Crete, the principal site of the
Minoan civilization which may
be equated with Plato's
Atlantis.

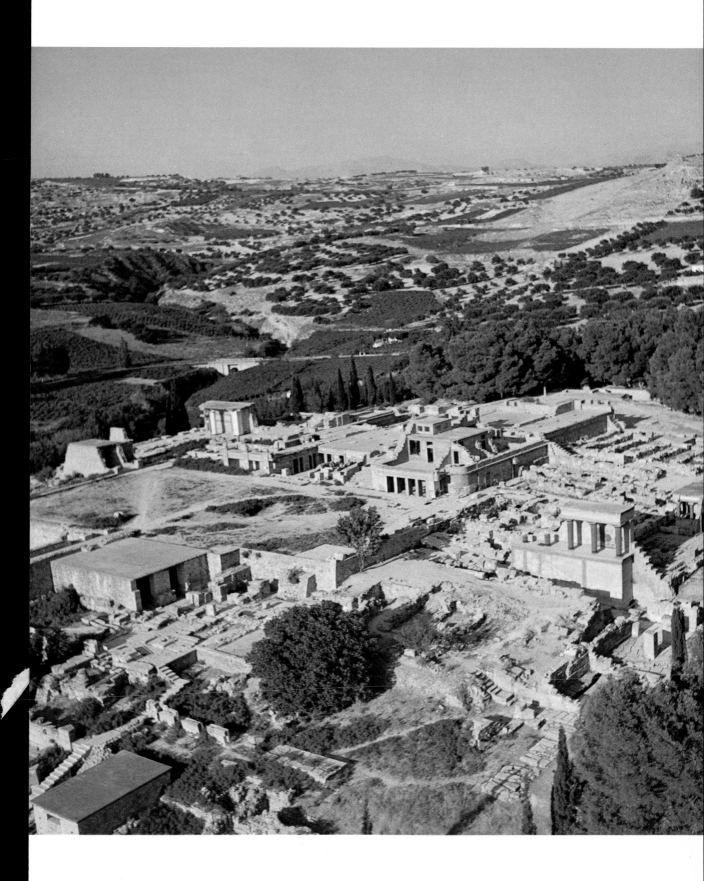

it is told, has the fashion of a legend, but the truth of it lies in the occurrence of a shifting of the bodies in the heavens which move round the earth, and a destruction of the things on the earth by fierce fire, which recurs at long intervals. At such times all they that dwell on the mountains and in high and dry places suffer destruction more than those who dwell near to rivers or the sea; and in our case the Nile, our Saviour in other ways, saves us also at such times from this calamity by rising high. And when, on the other hand, the Gods purge the earth with a flood of waters, all the herdsmen and shepherds that are in the mountains are saved, but those in the cities of your land are swept into the sea by the streams; whereas in our country neither then nor at any other time does the water pour down over our fields from above, on the contrary it all tends naturally to well up from below. Hence it is, for these reasons, that what is here preserved is reckoned to be most ancient; the truth being that in every place where there is no excessive heat or cold to prevent it there always exists some human stock, now more, now less in number. And if any event has occurred that is noble or great or in any way conspicuous, whether it be in your country or in ours or in some other place of which we know by report, all such events are recorded from of old and preserved here in our temples; whereas your people and the others are but newly equipped, every time, with letters and all such arts as civilized States require; and when, after the usual interval of years, like a plague, the flood from heaven comes sweeping down afresh upon your people, it leaves none of you but the unlettered and uncultured, so that you become young as ever, with no knowledge of all that happened in old times in this land or in your own. Certainly the genealogies which you related just now, Solon, concerning the people of your country, are little better than children's tales; for, in the first place, you remember but one deluge, though many had occurred previously; and next, you are ignorant of the fact that the noblest and most perfect race amongst men were born in the land where you now dwell, and from them both you yourself are sprung and the whole of your existing city, out of some little seed that chanced to be left over; but this has escaped your notice because for many generations the survivors died with no power to express themselves in writing. For verily at one time, Solon, before the greatest destruction by water, what is now the Athenian State was the bravest in war and supremely well organized also in all other respects. It is said that it possessed the most splendid works of art and the noblest polity of any nation under heaven of which we have heard tell.'

Upon hearing this, Solon said that he marvelled, and with the utmost eagerness requested the priest to recount for him in order and exactly all the facts about those citizens of old. The priest

23

then said: 'I begrudge you not the story, Solon; nay, I will tell it, both for your own sake and that of your city, and most of all for the sake of the Goddess who has adopted for her own both your land and this of ours, and has nurtured and trained them—yours first by the space of a thousand years, when she had received the

E seed of you from Gê and Hephaestus, and after that ours. And the duration of our civilization as set down in our sacred writings is 8,000 years. Of the citizens, then, who lived 9,000 years ago, I will declare to you briefly certain of their laws and the noblest of the deeds they performed: the full account in precise order and detail we shall go through later at our leisure, taking the actual writings. To get a view of their laws, look at the laws here; for you will find existing here at the present time many examples of the laws which then existed in your city. You see, first, how the priestly class is separated off from the rest; next, the class of craftsmen, of which each sort works by itself without mixing with any other; then the

B classes of shepherds, hunters, and farmers, each distinct and separate. Moreover, the military class here, as no doubt you have noticed, is kept apart from all the other classes, being enjoined by the law to devote itself solely to the work of training for war. A further feature is the character of their equipment with shields and spears; for we were the first of the peoples of Asia to adopt these weapons, it being the Goddess who instructed us, even as she instructed you first of all the dwellers in yonder lands. Again, with regard to wisdom, you perceive, no doubt, the law here—

C how much attention it has devoted from the very beginning to the Cosmic Order, by discovering all the effects which the divine causes produce upon human life, down to divination and the art of medicine which aims at health, and by its mastery also of all the other subsidiary studies. So when, at that time, the Goddess had furnished you, before all others, with all this orderly and regular system, she established your State, choosing the spot wherein you were born since she perceived therein a climate duly blended, and how that it would bring forth men of supreme

D wisdom. So it was that the Goddess, being herself both a lover of war and a lover of wisdom, chose the spot which was likely to bring forth men most like unto herself, and this first she established. Wherefore you lived under the rule of such laws as these— yea, and laws still better—and you surpassed all men in every virtue, as became those who were the offspring and nurslings of gods. Many, in truth, and great are the achievements of your State, which are a marvel to men as they are here recorded; but

E there is one which stands out above all both for magnitude and for nobleness. For it is related in our records how once upon a time your State stayed the course of a mighty host, which, starting from a distant point in the Atlantic ocean, was insolently advancing to attack the whole of Europe, and Asia to boot. For the ocean there was at that time navigable; for in front of the mouth which you Greeks call, as you say, "the pillars of Heracles", there lay an island which was larger than Libya and Asia together; and it was possible for the travellers of that time to cross from it to the other islands, and from the islands to the whole of the continent over

25   against them which encompasses that veritable ocean. For all that we have here, lying within the mouth of which we speak, is evidently a haven having a narrow entrance; but that yonder is a real ocean, and the land surrounding it may most rightly be called, in the fullest and truest sense, a continent. Now in this island of Atlantis, there existed a confederation of kings, of great and marvellous power, which held sway over all the island, and over many other islands also and parts of the continent; and, moreover, of the lands here within the Straits they ruled over

B   Libya as far as Egypt, and over Europe as far as Tuscany. So this host, being all gathered together, made an attempt one time to enslave by one single onslaught both your country and ours and the whole of the territory within the Straits. And then it was, Solon, that the manhood of your State showed itself conspicuous

C   for valour and might in the sight of all the world. For it stood pre-eminent above all in gallantry and all warlike arts, and acting partly as leader of the Greeks, and partly standing alone by itself when deserted by all others, after encountering the deadliest perils, it defeated the invaders and reared a trophy; whereby it saved from slavery such as were not as yet enslaved, and all the rest of us who dwell within the bounds of Heracles it ungrudgingly set free. But at a later time there occurred portentous earthquakes

D   and floods, and one grievous day and night befell them, when the whole body of your warriors was swallowed up by the earth, and the island of Atlantis in like manner was swallowed up by the sea and vanished; wherefore also the ocean at that spot has now become impassable and unsearchable, being blocked up by the shoal mud which the island created as it settled down.'

CRITIAS

108   CRIT. You, my dear Hermocrates, are posted in the last rank, with another man before you, so you are still courageous. But experience of our task will of itself speedily enlighten you as to its

D   character. However, I must trust to your consolation and encouragement, and in addition to the gods you mentioned I must call upon all the rest and especially upon Mnemosynê. For practically all the most important part of our speech depends upon this goddess; for if I can sufficiently remember and report the tale once told by the priests and brought hither by Solon, I am well-nigh convinced that I shall appear to the present audience to have fulfilled my task adequately. This, then, I must at once proceed to do, and procrastinate no longer.

E Now first of all we must recall the fact that 9,000 is the sum of years since the war occurred, as is recorded, between the dwellers beyond the pillars of Heracles and all that dwelt within them; which war we have now to relate in detail. It was stated that this city of ours was in command of the one side and fought through the whole of the war, and in command of the other side were the kings of the island of Atlantis, which we said was an island larger than Libya and Asia once upon a time, but now lies sunk by earthquakes and has created a barrier of impassable mud which prevents those who are sailing out from here to the ocean beyond from proceeding further. Now as regards the numerous barbaric tribes and all the Hellenic nations that then existed, the sequel of our story, when it is, as it were, unrolled, will disclose what happened in each locality; but the facts about the Athenians of that age and the enemies with whom they fought we must necessarily describe first, at the outset—the military power, that is to say, of each and their forms of government. And of these two we must give the priority in our account to the state of Athens.

B Once upon a time the gods were taking over by lot the whole earth according to its regions—not according to the results of strife: for it would not be reasonable to suppose that the gods were ignorant of their own several rights, nor yet that they attempted to obtain for themselves by means of strife a possession to which others, as they knew, had a better claim. So by just allotments they received each one his own, and they settled their countries; and when they had thus settled them, they reared us up, even as herdsmen rear their flocks, to be their cattle and nurslings; only it was not our bodies that they constrained by bodily force, like **C** shepherds guiding their flocks with stroke of staff, but they directed from the stern where the living creature is easiest to turn about, laying hold on the soul by persuasion, as by a rudder, according to their own disposition; and thus they drove and steered all the mortal kind. Now in other regions others of the gods had their allotments and ordered the affairs, but inasmuch as Hephaestus and Athena were of a like nature, being born of the same father, and agreeing, moreover, in their love of wisdom and of craftsmanship, they both took for their joint portion this land of ours as being naturally congenial and adapted for virtue **D** and for wisdom, and therein they planted as native to the soil men of virtue and ordained to their mind the mode of government. And of these citizens the names are preserved, but their works have vanished owing to the repeated destruction of their successors and the length of the intervening periods. For, as was said before, the stock that survived on each occasion was a remnant of unlettered mountaineers which had heard the names only of the rulers, and but little besides of their works. So though they gladly passed on

E these names to their descendants, concerning the mighty deeds and the laws of their predecessors they had no knowledge, save for some invariably obscure reports; and since, moreover, they and their children for many generations were themselves in want

110 of the necessaries of life, their attention was given to their own needs and all their talk was about them; and in consequence they paid no regard to the happenings of bygone ages. For legendary lore and the investigation of antiquity are visitants that come to cities in company with leisure, when they see that men are already furnished with the necessaries of life, and not before.

In this way, then, the names of the ancients, without their works, have been preserved. And for evidence of what I say I point to the statement of Solon, that the Egyptian priests, in describing the war of that period, mentioned most of those names

B —such as those of Cecrops and Erechtheus and Erichthonius and Erysichthon and most of the other names which are recorded of the various heroes before Theseus—and in like manner also the names of the women. Moreover, the habit and figure of the goddess

C indicate that in the case of all animals, male and female, that herd together, every species is naturally capable of practising as a whole and in common its own proper excellence.

Now at that time there dwelt in this country not only the other classes of the citizens who were occupied in the handicrafts and in the raising of food from the soil, but also the military class, which had been separated off at the commencement by divine heroes and dwelt apart. It was supplied with all that was required for its sustenance and training, and none of its members possessed any private property, but they regarded all they had as the

D common property of all; and from the rest of the citizens they claimed to receive nothing beyond a sufficiency of sustenance; and they practised all those pursuits which were mentioned yesterday, in the description of our proposed 'Guardians'. Moreover, what was related about our country was plausible and true, namely, that, in the first place, it had its boundaries at that time marked off by the Isthmus, and on the inland side reaching to the heights of Cithaeron and Parnes; and that the boundaries ran

E down with Oropia on the right, and on the seaward side they shut off the Asopus on the left; and that all other lands were surpassed by ours in goodness of soil, so that it was actually able at that period to support a large host which was exempt from the labours of husbandry. And of its goodness a strong proof is this: what is now left of our soil rivals any other in being all-productive and abundant in crops and rich in pasturage for all kinds of cattle; and at that period, in addition to their fine quality it produced these things in vast quantity. How, then, is this statement plausible, and what residue of the land then existing serves to confirm its truth? The whole of the land lies like a promontory jutting out from the rest of the continent far into the sea; and all the cup of the sea round about it is, as it happens, of a great depth. Consequently, since many great convulsions took place during

B the 9,000 years—for such was the number of years from that time to this—the soil which has kept breaking away from the high lands during these ages and these disasters, forms no pile of sediment worth mentioning, as in other regions, but keeps sliding away ceaselessly and disappearing in the deep. And, just as happens in small islands, what now remains compared with what then existed is like the skeleton of a sick man, all the fat and soft earth having wasted away, and only the bare framework of the land being left. But at that epoch the country was unimpaired,

C and for its mountains it had high arable hills, and in place of the 'moorlands', as they are now called, it contained plains full of rich soil; and it had much forest-land in its mountains, of which there are visible signs even to this day; for there are some mountains which now have nothing but food for bees, but they had trees no very long time ago, and the rafters from those felled there to roof the largest buildings are still sound. And besides, there were many lofty trees of cultivated species; and it produced boundless pasturage for flocks. Moreover, it was enriched by the

D yearly rains from Zeus, which were not lost to it, as now, by flowing from the bare land into the sea; but the soil it had was deep, and therein it received the water, storing it up in the retentive loamy soil; and by drawing off into the hollows from the heights the water that was there absorbed, it provided all the various districts with abundant supplies of spring-waters and streams, whereof the shrines which still remain even now, at the spots where the fountains formerly existed, are signs which testify that our present description of the land is true.

E Such, then, was the natural condition of the rest of the country, and it was ornamented as you would expect from genuine husbandmen who made husbandry their sole task, and who were also men of taste and of native talent, and possessed of most excellent land and a great abundance of water, and also, above the land, a climate of most happily tempered seasons. And as to the city, this is the way in which it was laid out at that time. In the first place, the Acropolis, as it existed then, was different from

what it is now. For as it is now, the action of a single night of extraordinary rain has crumbled it away and made it bare of soil, when earthquakes occurred simultaneously with the third of the disastrous floods which preceded the destructive deluge in the time of Deucalion. But in its former extent, at an earlier period, it went down towards the Eridanus and the Ilissus, and embraced within it the Pnyx, and had the Lycabettus as its boundary over against the Pnyx; and it was all rich in soil and, save for a small

B space, level on the top. And its outer parts, under its slopes, were inhabited by the craftsmen and by such of the husbandmen as had their farms close by; but on the topmost part only the military class by itself had its dwellings round about the temple of Athene and Hephaestus, surrounding themselves with a single ring-fence, which formed, as it were, the enclosure of a single dwelling. On the northward side of it they had established their public dwellings and winter mess-rooms, and all the arrangements in the way of buildings which were required for the community

C life of themselves and the priests; but all was devoid of gold or silver, of which they made no use anywhere; on the contrary, they aimed at the mean between luxurious display and meanness, and built themselves tasteful houses, wherein they and their children's children grew old and handed them on in succession unaltered to others like themselves. As for the southward parts, when they vacated their gardens and gymnasia and mess-rooms as was natural in summer, they used them for these purposes. And near

D the place of the present Acropolis there was one spring—which was choked up by the earthquakes so that but small tricklings of it are now left round about; but to the men of that time it afforded a plentiful stream for them all, being well tempered both for winter and summer. In this fashion, then, they dwelt, acting as guardians of their own citizens and as leaders, by their own consent, of the rest of the Greeks; and they watched carefully that their own numbers, of both men and women, who were neither too young nor too old to fight, should remain for all times as nearly as possible the same, namely, about 20,000.

E So it was that these men, being themselves of the character described and always justly administering in some such fashion both their own land and Hellas, were famous throughout all Europe and Asia both for their bodily beauty and for the perfection of their moral excellence, and were of all men then living the most renowned. And now, if we have not lost recollection of what we heard when we were still children, we will frankly impart to you all, as friends, our story of the men who warred against our Athenians, what their state was and how it originally came about.

But before I begin my account, there is still a small point which I ought to explain, lest you should be surprised at frequently hearing Greek names given to barbarians. The reason of this you shall now learn. Since Solon was planning to make use of the story for his own poetry, he had found, on investigating the meaning of the names, that those Egyptians who had first written them down had translated them into their own tongue. So he himself in turn recovered the original sense of each name and, rendering

B it into our tongue, wrote it down so. And these very writings were in the possession of my grandfather and are actually now in mine, and when I was a child I learnt them all by heart. Therefore if the names you hear are just like our local names, do not be at all astonished; for now you know the reason for them. The story then told was a long one, and it began something like this.

Like as we previously stated concerning the allotments of the Gods, that they portioned out the whole earth, here into larger allotments and there into smaller, and provided for themselves

C shrines and sacrifices, even so Poseidon took for his allotment the island of Atlantis and settled therein the children whom he had begotten of a mortal woman in a region of the island of the following description. Bordering on the sea and extending through the centre of the whole island there was a plain, which is said to have been the fairest of all plains and highly fertile; and, moreover, near the plain, over against its centre, at a distance of about 50 stades, there stood a mountain that was low on all sides. Thereon dwelt one of the natives originally sprung from the earth,

D Evenor by name, with his wife Leucippe; and they had for offspring an only-begotten daughter, Cleito. And when this damsel was now come to marriageable age, her mother died and also her father; and Poseidon, being smitten with desire for her, wedded her; and to make the hill whereon she dwelt impregnable he broke it off all round about; and he made circular belts of sea and land enclosing one another alternately, some greater, some smaller, two being of land and three of sea, which he carved as it were out of the midst of the island; and these belts were at even distances

E on all sides, so as to be impassable for man; for at that time neither ships nor sailing were as yet in existence. And Poseidon himself set in order with ease, as a god would, the central island, bringing up from beneath the earth two springs of waters, the one flowing warm from its source, the other cold, and producing out of the earth all kinds of food in plenty. And he begat five pairs of twin sons and reared them up; and when he had divided all the island of Atlantis into ten portions, he assigned to the first-born of the

114   eldest sons his mother's dwelling and the allotment surrounding it, which was the largest and best; and him he appointed to be king over the rest, and the others to be rulers, granting to each the rule over many men and a large tract of country. And to all of them he gave names, giving to him that was eldest and king the name after which the whole island was called and the sea spoken of as the Atlantic, because the first king who then reigned had the name of Atlas. And the name of his younger twin-brother, who

B had for his portion the extremity of the island near the pillars of Heracles up to the part of the country now called Gadeira after the name of that region, was Eumelus in Greek, but in the native tongue Gadeirus—which fact may have given its title to the country. And of the pair that were born next he called the one Ampheres and the other Evaemon; and of the third pair the elder

C was named Mneseus and the younger Autochthon; and of the fourth pair, he called the first Elasippus and the second Mestor; and of the fifth pair, Azaes was the name given to the elder, and Diaprepês to the second. So all these, themselves and their descendants, dwelt for many generations bearing rule over many other islands throughout the sea, and holding sway besides, as was previously stated, over the Mediterranean peoples as far as Egypt and Tuscany.

Now a large family of distinguished sons sprang from Atlas;

D but it was the eldest, who, as king, always passed on the sceptre to the eldest of his sons, and thus they preserved the sovereignty for many generations; and the wealth they possessed was so immense that the like had never been seen before in any royal house nor will ever easily be seen again; and they were provided with everything of which provision was needed either in the city or throughout the rest of the country. For because of their headship

E they had a large supply of imports from abroad, and the island itself furnished most of the requirements of daily life—metals, to begin with, both the hard kind and the fusible kind, which are extracted by mining, and also that kind which is now known only by name but was more than a name then, there being mines of it in many places of the island—I mean 'orichalcum', which was the most precious of the metals then known, except gold. It brought forth also in abundance all the timbers that a forest provides for the labours of carpenters; and of animals it produced a sufficiency, both of tame and wild. Moreover, it contained a very large stock of elephants; for there was an ample food-supply not only for all the other animals which haunt the marshes and lakes

115 and rivers, or the mountains or the plains, but likewise also for this animal, which of its nature is the largest and most voracious. And in addition to all this, it produced and brought to perfection all those sweet-scented stuffs which the earth produces now, whether made of roots or herbs or trees, or of liquid gums derived from flowers or fruits. The cultivated fruit also, and the dry, which serves us for nutriment, and all the other kinds that we use for our meals—the various species of which are comprehended

B under the name 'vegetables'—and all the produce of trees which affords liquid and solid food and unguents, and the fruit of the orchard-trees, so hard to store, which is grown for the sake of amusement and pleasure, and all the after-dinner fruits that we serve up as welcome remedies for the sufferer from repletion—all these that hallowed island, as it lay then beneath the sun, produced in marvellous beauty and endless abundance. And thus, receiving from the earth all these products, they furnished forth

C their temples and royal dwellings, their harbours and their docks, and all the rest of their country, ordering all in the fashion following.

First of all they bridged over the circles of sea which surrounded the ancient metropolis, making thereby a road towards and from the royal palace. And they had built the palace at the very beginning where the settlement was first made by their God and their ancestors; and as each king received it from his predecessor,

D he added to its adornment and did all he could to surpass the king before him, until finally they made of it an abode amazing to behold for the magnitude and beauty of its workmanship. For, beginning at the sea, they bored a channel right through to the outermost circle, which was three plethra in breadth, one hundred feet in depth, and fifty stades in length; and thus they made the entrance to it from the sea like that to a harbour by opening out a mouth large enough for the greatest ships to sail through. More-

E over, through the circles of land, which divided those of sea, over against the bridges they opened out a channel leading from circle to circle, large enough to give passage to a single trireme; and this they roofed over above so that the sea-way was subterranean; for the lips of the land-circles were raised a sufficient height above the level of the sea. The greatest of the circles into which a boring was made for the sea was three stades in breadth, and the circle of land next to it was of equal breadth; and of the second pair of circles that of water was two stades in breadth and that of dry land equal again to the preceding one of water; and the circle which ran round the central island itself was of a stade's breadth.

116 And this island, wherein stood the royal palace, was of five stades in diameter. Now the island and the circles and the bridge, which was a plethrum in breadth, they encompassed round about, on this side and on that, with a wall of stone; and upon the bridges on each side, over against the passages for the sea, they erected towers and gates. And the stone they quarried beneath the central island all round, and from beneath the outer and inner circles,

B some of it being white, some black and some red; and while quarrying it they constructed two inner docks, hollowed out and roofed over by the native rock. And of the buildings some they framed of one simple colour, in others they wove a pattern of many colours by blending the stones for the sake of ornament so as to confer upon the buildings a natural charm. And they covered with brass, as though with a plaster, all the circumference of the wall which surrounded the outermost circle; and that of the

inner one they coated with tin; and that which encompassed the
C acropolis itself with orichalcum which sparkled like fire.

The royal palace within the acropolis was arranged in this manner. In the centre there stood a temple sacred to Cleito and Poseidon, which was reserved as holy ground, and encircled with a wall of gold; this being the very spot where at the beginning they had generated and brought to birth the family of the ten royal lines. Thither also they brought year by year from all the ten allotments their seasonable offerings to do sacrifice to each
D of those princes. And the temple of Poseidon himself was a stade in length, three plethra in breadth, and of a height which appeared symmetrical therewith; and there was something of the barbaric in its appearance. All the exterior of the temple they coated with silver, save only the pinnacles, and these they coated with gold. As to the interior, they made the roof all of ivory in appearance, variegated with gold and silver and orichalcum, and all the rest of the walls and pillars and floors they covered with orichalcum. And they placed therein golden statues, one being
E that of the God standing on a chariot and driving six winged steeds, his own figure so tall as to touch the ridge of the roof, and round about him a hundred Nereids on dolphins (for that was the number of them as men then believed); and it contained also many other images, the votive offerings of private men. And outside, round about the temple, there stood images in gold of all the princes, both themselves and their wives, as many as were descended from the ten kings, together with many other votive offerings both of the kings and of private persons not only from the State itself but also from all the foreign peoples over whom
they ruled. And the altar, in respect of its size and its workmanship, harmonized with its surroundings; and the royal palace likewise was such as befitted the greatness of the kingdom, and equally befitted the splendour of the temples.

The springs they made use of, one kind being of cold, another of warm water, were of abundant volume, and each kind was wonderfully well adapted for use because of the natural taste and excellence of its waters; and these they surrounded with buildings
B and with plantations of trees such as suited the waters; and, moreover, they set reservoirs round about, some under the open sky, and others under cover to supply hot baths in the winter; they put separate baths for the kings and for the private citizens, besides others for women, and others again for horses and all other beasts of burden, fitting out each in an appropriate manner. And the outflowing water they conducted to the sacred grove of Poseidon, which contained trees of all kinds that were of marvellous beauty and height because of the richness of the soil; and by means of channels they led the water to the outer circles over

against the bridges. And there they had constructed many

C temples for gods, and many gardens and many exercising grounds, some for men and some set apart for horses, in each of the circular belts of island; and besides the rest they had in the centre of the large island a racecourse laid out for horses, which was a stade in width, while as to length, a strip which ran round the whole circumference was reserved for equestrian contests. And round about it, on this side and on that, were barracks for the greater part of the spearmen; but the guard-house of the more

D trusty of them was posted in the smaller circle, which was nearer the acropolis; while those who were the most trustworthy of all had dwellings granted to them within the acropolis round about the persons of the kings.

And the shipyards were full of triremes and all the tackling that belongs to triremes, and they were all amply equipped.

Such then was the state of things round about the abode of the

E kings. And after crossing the three outer harbours, one found a wall which began at the sea and ran round in a circle, at a uniform distance of fifty stades from the largest circle and harbour, and its ends converged at the seaward mouth of the channel. The whole of this wall had numerous houses built on to it, set close together; while the sea-way and the largest harbour were filled with ships and merchants coming from all quarters, which by reason of their multitude caused clamour and tumult of every description and an unceasing din night and day.

Now as regards the city and the environs of the ancient dwelling we have now wellnigh completed the description as it was origin-

ally given. We must endeavour next to repeat the account of the rest of the country, what its natural character was, and in what fashion it was ordered. In the first place, then, according to the account, the whole region rose sheer out of the sea to a great height, but the part about the city was all a smooth plain, enclosing it round about, and being itself encircled by mountains which stretched as far as to the sea; and this plain had a level surface and was as a whole rectangular in shape, being 3,000 stades long on either side and 2,000 stades wide at its centre, reckoning upwards from the sea. And this region, all along the island, faced

B towards the South and was sheltered from the Northern blasts. And the mountains which surrounded it were at that time celebrated as surpassing all that now exist in number, magnitude and beauty; for they had upon them many rich villages of country folk, and streams and lakes and meadows which furnished ample nutriment to all the animals both tame and wild, and timber of various sizes and descriptions, abundantly sufficient for the needs of all and every craft.

C Now as a result of natural forces, together with the labours of many kings which extended over many ages, the condition of the plain was this. It was originally a quadrangle, rectilinear for the most part, and elongated; and what it lacked of this shape they made right by means of a trench dug round about it. Now, as regards the depth of this trench and its breadth and length, it seems incredible that it should be so large as the account states, considering that it was made by hand, and in addition to all the other operations, but none the less we must report what we heard: it was dug out to the depth of a plethrum and to a uniform

D breadth of a stade, and since it was dug round the whole plain its consequent length was 10,000 stades. It received the streams which came down from the mountains and after circling round the plain, and coming towards the city on this side and on that, it discharged them thereabouts into the sea. And on the inland side of the city channels were cut in straight lines, of about 100 feet in width, across the plain, and these discharged themselves into the trench on the seaward side, the distance between each being 100 stades. It was in this way that they conveyed to the city the timber

E from the mountains and transported also on boats the seasons' products, by cutting transverse passages from one channel to the next and also to the city. And they cropped the land twice a year, making use of the rains from Heaven in the winter, and the waters that issue from the earth in summer, by conducting the streams from the trenches.

As regards their man-power, it was ordained that each allotment should furnish one man as leader of all the men in the plain who were fit to bear arms; and the size of the allotment was about ten times ten stades, and the total number of all the allotments was 60,000; and the number of the men in the mountains and in the rest of the country was countless, according to the report, and according to their districts and villages they were all assigned to these allotments under their leaders. So it was ordained that each such leader should provide for war the sixth part of a war-chariot's equipment, so as to make up 10,000 chariots in all, together with

B two horses and mounted men; also a pair of horses without a car, and attached thereto a combatant with a small shield and for charioteer the rider who springs from horse to horse; and two hoplites; and archers and slingers, two of each; and light-armed slingers and javelin-men, three of each; and four sailors towards the manning of twelve hundred ships. Such then were the military dispositions of the royal City; and those of the other nine varied in various ways, which it would take a long time to tell.

C Of the magistracies and posts of honour the disposition, ever since the beginning, was this. Each of the ten kings ruled over the men and most of the laws in his own particular portion and throughout his own city, punishing and putting to death whomsoever he willed. But their authority over one another and their mutual relations were governed by the precepts of Poseidon, as handed down to them by the law and by the records inscribed by the first princes on a pillar of orichalcum, which was placed within

D the temple of Poseidon in the centre of the island; and thither they assembled every fifth year, and then alternately every sixth year—giving equal honour to both the even and the odd—and when thus assembled they took counsel about public affairs and inquired if any had in any way transgressed and gave judgement. And when they were about to give judgement they first gave pledges one to another of the following description. In the sacred precincts of Poseidon there were bulls at large; and the ten princes, being alone by themselves, after praying to the God that they

E might capture a victim well-pleasing unto him, hunted after the bulls with staves and nooses but with no weapon of iron; and whatsoever bull they captured they led up to the pillar and cut its throat over the top of the pillar, raining down blood on the inscription. And inscribed upon the pillar, besides the laws, was an oath which invoked mighty curses upon them that disobeyed. When then, they had done sacrifice according to their laws and

were consecrating all the limbs of the bull, they mixed a bowl of wine and poured in on behalf of each one a gout of blood, and the rest they carried to the fire, when they had first purged the pillars round about. And after this they drew out from the bowl with golden ladles, and making libation over the fire swore to give judgement according to the laws upon the pillar and to punish whosoever had committed any previous transgression; and, moreover, that henceforth they would not transgress any of the writings

B willingly, nor govern nor submit to any governor's edict save in accordance with their father's laws. And when each of them had made this invocation both for himself and for his seed after him, he drank of the cup and offered it up as a gift in the temple of the God; and after spending the interval in supping and necessary business, when darkness came on and the sacrificial fire had died down, all the princes robed themselves in most beautiful sable vestments, and sat on the ground beside the cinders of the sacramental victims throughout the night, extinguishing all the

C fire that was round about the sanctuary; and there they gave and received judgement, if any of them accused any of committing any transgression. And when they had given judgement, they wrote the judgements, when it was light, upon a golden tablet, and dedicated them together with their robes as memorials. And there were many other special laws concerning the peculiar rights of the several princes, whereof the most important were these: that they should never take up arms against one another, and that, should anyone attempt to overthrow in any city their royal house, they should all lend aid, taking counsel in common, like

D their forerunners, concerning their policy in war and other matters, while conceding the leadership to the royal branch of Atlas; and that the king had no authority to put to death any of his brother-princes save with the consent of more than half of the ten.

Such was the magnitude and character of the power which existed in those regions at that time; and this power the God set in array and brought against these regions of ours on some such pretext as the following, according to the story. For many genera-

E tions, so long as the inherited nature of the God remained strong in them, they were submissive to the laws and kindly disposed to their divine kindred. For the intents of their hearts were true and in all ways noble, and they showed gentleness joined with wisdom in dealing with the changes and chances of life and in their dealings one with another. Consequently they thought scorn of everything save virtue and lightly esteemed their rich possessions,

121 bearing with ease the burden, as it were, of the vast volume of their gold and other goods; and thus their wealth did not make them drunk with pride so that they lost control of themselves and went to ruin; rather, in their soberness of mind they clearly saw that all these good things are increased by general amity combined with virtue, whereas the eager pursuit and worship of these goods not only causes the goods themselves to diminish but makes virtue also to perish with them. As a result, then, of such reasoning and of the continuance of their divine nature all their wealth had grown to such a greatness as we previously described. But when the portion of divinity within them was now becoming faint and weak through being ofttimes blended with a large measure of

B mortality, whereas the human temper was becoming dominant, then at length they lost their comeliness, through being unable to bear the burden of their possessions, and became ugly to look upon, in the eyes of him who has the gift of sight; for they had lost the fairest of their goods from the most precious of their parts; but in the eyes of those who have no gift of perceiving what is the truly happy life, it was then above all that they appeared to be superlatively fair and blessed, filled as they were with lawless ambition and power. And Zeus, the God of gods, who reigns by Law, inasmuch as he has the gift of perceiving such things, marked how this righteous race was in evil plight, and desired to inflict punishment upon them, to the end that when chastised

C they might strike a truer note. Wherefore he assembled together all the gods into that abode which they honour most, standing as it does at the centre of all the Universe, and beholding all things that partake of generation; and when he had assembled them, he spake thus: . . .

Appendix B

In the main body of the book we have been concerned primarily with the effects of the Santorin eruption and the collapse of the central part of the island on Santorin itself, Crete and Athens, and the parallel fate of Atlantis. It is, however, more than likely that such an unprecedented cataclysm should have affected a wider area of the Eastern Mediterranean; and it is interesting, and possibly rewarding, to examine the evidence or traditions of other perhaps contemporary disasters which can also be explained as by-products of the Santorin explosion.

The one which first comes to mind is, of course, Deucalion's Flood, which reputedly affected the whole mainland of Greece, notably Thessaly, Phthia, Boeotia, Attica, Argolis, Elis, Aetolia, Epirus, such Aegean islands as Lesbos, Chios, Crete and Rhodes, and in general, the East Mediterranean coasts from Lycia to Sicily. A tablet found at Ras Shamra (ancient Ugarit) gives a graphic account of one of the waves which seem to have occurred on the Syrian coast in the Second Millennium BC. Another Ras Shamra tablet tells a similar story of a catastrophic earthquake followed by a seismic sea-wave which levelled the port of Ugarit around 1370 BC. Lack of rapid communication and the destruction of coastwise shipping together with the uniformity of the phenomena could be reasons for the flood being considered a local disaster and each of the places affected as the starting point of a local deluge rather than a common sufferer in a general disaster. This pseudo-local explanation together with the fact that the Santorin disaster had several phases could be a reason for the conflicting dates ascribed to the different aspects.

The traditions of the Flood are, not surprisingly, confused and confusing. It has been variously assigned to the time of Cranaos, King of Athens, and Triopa of Marathon, to the time of Ogyges, of Aethlios of Elis, of Orestheus of Aetolia, of Lycaon of Arcadia and the times of Cecrops and Moses. According to the Saite priest (in Plato) the destruction of Attica happened after the war between the Athenians and the islanders of Atlantis. Since, according to this priest, this war was waged under Erysichthon, son of Cecrops and grandson of Erechtheus, the Flood of Deucalion must have occurred during or after their reign. Cecrops is traditionally the seventh king of Athens and was succeeded by Cranaos, who had three daughters, Cranae, Cranaechme and Atthis—after whom the region was named Atthis or Attica.

PLATE 21. An explosive burst from Surtsey, where pyroclastic (solid) ejecta appeared along with flows of lava.

Overleaf PLATE 22. A volcanic caldera which resembles that of Santorin in the most important respects is that of Crater Lake, in Oregon, USA. It was formed by a cataclysmic eruption of Mount Mazama, approximately 6,500 years ago. These paintings by Paul Rockwood, based on scientific data, are reconstructions of the summit of Mount Mazama before the eruption and of the crater formed by the explosion or subsidence of the mountain's summit.

Overleaf, facing page PLATE 23. A view of part of Crater Lake today.

These loose traditions, however, have been linked by early Christian historians with the Exodus of the Israelites. According to A. Stagerites, Deucalion was born in 1573 BC and reigned in 1541 BC while the Flood took place in 1529 BC; and Velikovsky mentions that according to Seth Calvisius, Deucalion's Flood took place in 1516 BC, but in 1511 BC according to Christopher Helvicus. There are in fact many indications that Deucalion's Flood was contemporary with the collapse of Santorin and the consequent huge *tsunamis* which devastated the East Mediterranean coasts. Relying on the chronology of Calvisius and Helvicus, Velikovsky believes that Deucalion's Flood and the Exodus of the Israelites took place at precisely the same time. These authorities claim that the Exodus took place in 1495 BC. Professor P. Bratsiotis maintains that the Exodus took place most probably in the reign of Amenophis II (1457–1426 BC) and not during that of Merenptah (1246–1239), as was formerly maintained (and indeed still is) by some scholars.

Biblical scholars have now for many years supported the view that the Israelites crossed, not the Red Sea, but the Sea of Reeds. The words *Jam Suf* are usually translated 'Red Sea' but there are many who suggest that *Suf* means 'reed'. If this is accepted, *Jam Suf* must have been a lake or lagoon, since reeds do not grow in salt water. An inscription found at El Arish, referring to a great Egyptian disaster, supports the view that the Sea of Reeds was the Sirbonis Lake—the lagoon between the towns of Romani and El Arish to the east of the Nile delta.[1] This lagoon, which lies parallel with the Mediterranean and Mt Kassion, was called Sirbon or the Sirbonis Lake in antiquity, and is now known as Sebcha el-Bardawil. It is mentioned in Herodotus as the boundary of Egypt, in whose depths the mythological giant, Typhon, dwelt. Strabo gave its maximum length as 200 stades (22 miles) and its breadth as 50 stades ($5\frac{1}{2}$ miles), and said that it was separated from the Mediterranean by a narrow sandy strip and that the lake communicated with the sea through a passage named Ekregma (gap). Strabo also stated that it was extremely dangerous to cross the lake, while Diodorus Siculus maintained that 'many who were ignorant of the features of the place were lost together with whole armies'.

If this view is accepted and the Exodus is indeed contemporary with Deucalion's Flood, the destruction of the Egyptian army could easily be one of the consequences of the *tsunami* generated by the collapse of the central part of Santorin, in the following manner. When the huge caldera was created by that collapse, the sea rushed in to fill the cauldron-like cavity—the present bay of Thera. As a result the water ebbed away from all the East Mediterranean coasts. As the sea withdrew, the strip dividing the lagoon from the sea would certainly widen, the 'gap' would cease to

PLATE 24. The most violent volcanic eruption of recent times, closely resembling the great eruption of Santorin, was that of Krakatoa, an island between Java and Sumatra, in the summer of 1883. This engraving was made from a photograph taken in May 1883, at an early stage of the eruption, and was coloured by an eyewitness; it was printed in the report of a committee set up by the Royal Society to investigate the eruption, published in 1888. It is the only known contemporary picture of the Krakatoa eruption in progress.

[1]Other scholars suggest that the 'Sea of Reeds' was the Lagoon of Manzala, just east of Raamses (Tanis), which was one of the cities built by the Israelites (Exodus 1.11). Whether we accept the Lagoon of Manzala or the Sirbonis Lake, the mechanism of the crossing shortly to be advanced is equally valid.

exist and the lagoon for a while become completely separated from the sea. The Israelites, taking advantage of this opportunity, would then have been able to cross the lagoon, or, more precisely, pass over the new piece of dry land suddenly created at the gap mentioned by Strabo. In fact, as stated in Exodus 14.22, 'the children of Israel went into the midst of the sea upon dry ground; and the waters were a wall unto them on their right hand, and on their left'.

The Hebrew text refers to 600,000 Israelites setting out from Egypt. This number seems extremely large, and some Jewish scholars, including David Ben-Gurion the former Prime Minister of Israel, have advanced the theory that there is a numerical error and that the Exodus comprised only 600 souls. Ancient references, particularly to the capture of prisoners, are usually grossly exaggerated. A typical example is found on the inscribed royal mace of the First Dynasty (3200–2900 BC) now in the Ashmolean Collection at Oxford. This refers to the capture of 120,000 prisoners, 400,000 oxen and 1,422,000 goats. Generally 'in dealing with old writers we have to reckon with their occasional wish to astound us, and must be on our guard against the human tendency to make things

The Sea of Reeds, which may be the route taken by the Israelites under Moses in the Exodus from Egypt.

interesting by additions'. In any case the discrepancy is made apparent by the relatively small force of Egyptians—600 chariots—sent out in pursuit.

Normally *tsunamis* appear between 15 and 30 minutes after the receding of the sea. In this period of time the smaller number of Israelites (as surmised from the number of Egyptian chariots sent out to pursue them) would be able to run over the piece of dry land temporarily created in the place of the gap; while the sea-wave that swept in after their passage would wipe out the Egyptians who 'pursued and went in after them to the midst of the sea, even all Pharaoh's horses, his chariots and his horsemen' (Exodus 14.24).

There are recorded parallels for such occurrences. During the winter of 479 BC a seismic wave occurred at Potidaea, in Chalcidice, a little south-east of modern Salonica. 'The initial ebb of the sea was so intense and lasted so long that an army seizing Potidaea had sufficient time to fall in rank and advance nearly a mile, by-passing the city from the sea-side which under normal conditions was inaccessible and was protected by deep waters. Then, the sea returning with great swell, overflooded the coast and drowned the advancing army.' In the Grand Banks earthquake of 18 November 1929 'the postmaster on seeing the sea retreat and leave the harbour bottom exposed, realized that it would return to a height equal to the depth to which it receded. In the few minutes before this occurred, he had time to run the length of the village's one street, calling to the people to flee to the hill, which they did, so that all were saved'. During the Chilean earthquake on 22 May 1960, the inhabitants of the coastal towns noted 'that the sea was beginning to retreat from the shores, exposing the ocean floor to distances well beyond the lowest tides. When this happened, the fire alarms were sounded, and firemen systematically went through the streets warning everyone of the impending danger. The people fled afoot and on horseback to the hills and waited. Those on horseback made repeated trips to save the old and infirm. After 15 to 30 minutes, the sea returned, advancing upon the shore in a wave that was, in places, over 20 feet high. The wave rushed over the land, covering and carrying away the houses, killing the animals that could not be evacuated, and carrying off some of the people who, for one reason or another, had not left their homes'. According to Professor Takahasi, President of the Tsunami Committee of the International Union of Geodesy and Geophysics, former Director, Earthquake Research Institute, Tokyo, 'the predominating peaks [in the spectra of *tsunamis*] fall into bands of periods of 84 min and 58 min when the magnitude of the earthquake and accordingly the magnitude of the *tsunami* is large, while the peaks of the shorter period of 28 min and 21 min are liable to appear when the magnitude of the earthquake is small'.

It is true that the route taken by the Israelites is not well established, but it seems reasonable that Moses would choose a less used route and a more difficult one in order to avoid or at any rate complicate pursuit by

an Egyptian army. The obvious route in these circumstances would be the sandy strip which separates the lagoon from the Mediterranean rather than the more direct one to the south or landward side of the lagoon. It should be mentioned that the withdrawal of the waters during *tsunamis* occurs at least three times and the second wave is usually the strongest. This would account for the time available for the Israelites to pass over a gap about 500 yds wide and for the destruction of the pursuing Egyptian army. Only one gap is mentioned in ancient accounts of the lagoon; and it can be surmised that Moses was unaware of the existence of this gap and that the raising of his hand when confronted by waters lying across his route had its origin in dismay and embarrassment.

This view that the Egyptians were destroyed in the Sirbonis lake by a seismic wave from the Mediterranean was put forward by Professor A. Sieberg in 1932, but he believed that it took place in March or April 1220 BC. The view previously held that the water of the lagoon was swept from the region of the gap by the blast of a strong east wind cannot be accepted for two reasons. First: because it seems improbable that wind energy could be sufficient to move such a large mass of water; and secondly: because a mass of water, driven by an east wind, would have blocked the western entry to the sandy strip of land and so made it impassable to the Israelites. True, Exodus 14.21 does state that the water was driven back by a strong east wind, but this is not exclusive. The wind could well be a concomitant of the *tsunami* and could accompany without causing the withdrawal of the waters brought about by the *tsunami*.

Recently J. C. Bennett, Director of the Institute for the Comparative Study of History, Philosophy and the Sciences, has reached some further conclusions based on additional evidence. He has shown that the prodigious eruption of Santorin was responsible not only for Deucalion's Flood and the destruction of Atlantis but also for the plagues of Egypt which made the Exodus possible.

The ten plagues of Egypt are referred to in the Bible as follows (Exodus 7–11):

1 The waters turned into blood
2 Frogs covering the land
3 Lice afflicting man and beast
4 Swarms of flies
5 Murrain attacking livestock
6 Boils and blains
7 Thunder and hail
8 Locusts
9 Darkness
10 Death of the first-born

If these calamities, which preceded the Exodus, are contemporary with the great eruption of Santorin, they may all be considered as direct or indirect consequences of it.

A small *tsunami* photographed in the harbour of Patmos. The water first withdraws (*upper picture*), then returns in the form of a seismic wave some minutes later.

Volcanic eruptions are usually triggered by great earthquakes. One of the chief major effects which accompany great earthquakes is the disturbance of ground and surface water dispositions. Earth slumping makes water muddy; landslides dam and divert streams and form lakes, pools and marshes; stagnant water, particularly in warm countries, is a breeding-ground for disease-carrying insects, particularly the *Anopheles* mosquito, which brings malaria. The fall of volcanic dust can bring about the complete failure of crops. The natural consequences of such effects are the disturbance of sanitary arrangements and the appearance of lice, the development of boils and blains, the death of men and animals from famine, swarms of flies from unburied corpses and carcases, and inroads of locusts and similar pests into areas perhaps less affected by the fall of volcanic dust.

That such effects can follow volcanic phenomena is well attested by similar events in historical times. On 8 June 1783, tremendous explosions of Mt Skaptar in Iceland, 200 miles east of Reykjavik, were accompanied by vast clouds of ash which fell over a wide area, even damaging crops in Scotland and Norway. Bullard states that:

'Although the lava flows caused great damage, even more serious was the bluish haze (probably containing SO_2) that lay over the country during the summer of 1783. It stunted the grass growth, causing a disastrous famine, still referred to as the Haze Famine. Hunger and disease, following the catastrophe, took their toll of human life. As a result of the eruption, Iceland lost one-fifth of its population, about three-fourths of its sheep and horses and one-half of its cattle (230,000 head). It was a national disaster from which it took years for the country to recover.'

A similar event happened in Java after the great earthquake and volcanic eruption of Tambora mountain on 10 April 1815. J. C. Bennett quotes from Sir Stamford Raffles' account of the event:

'. . . in Banyuwangi, the part of the island on which the cloud of ashes spent its force, the injury was more extensive. A large quantity of paddy was totally destroyed, and all the plantations more or less injured. 126 horses and 86 head of cattle also perished, chiefly for want of forage, during a month from the time of the eruption . . .'

In all violent eruptions there are thunderstorms with brilliant lightning, hail and heavy rain. The great heat in some eruptions also causes tornadoes. During the Tambora eruption of 1815 men, horses, cattle and anything moveable were snatched up, and large trees were torn out of the ground by the roots and whirled into the air. A tornado passing over rivers and freshwater lakes can lift live fish and frogs. The story of clouds 'raining frogs' is widespread. The French News Agency cabled from Ankara on 11 February 1963 that after a torrential fall of rain the streets of the Turkish town of Mersina were covered with small frogs. According to the same news agency a fall of frogs had been reported from the same town some time previously.

The darkening of the sky, the fall of hail and of red rain are not unusual in volcanic eruptions. It will be remembered that the first layer of pumice on Santorin is rose-coloured. Volcanic ash carried by high-level winds towards Egypt would fall on surface water and the iron oxide in the ash would dissolve in the waters and colour them red. Clouds of dust raised to high altitudes during the climax of the eruption would screen the sun and the sudden fall of temperature would result in cloudbursts and hailstorms. The death of the first-born gains its poignancy from the special values set by the Israelites on first-born sons; and, in point of fact (Exodus 11), although the death of the first-born is threatened by Moses, the text does not state that it actually took place.

If we assume that the plagues of Egypt were a by-product of the Santorin eruption, we may then go on to conclude that during the eruption the wind was blowing from the north-west and that the eruption took place in the summer when the Etesian or north-west winds are the prevailing winds in the Eastern Mediterranean. Recent research on the distribution of Santorin tephra (or volcanic ash) in the post-Pleistocene sediments in the Eastern Mediterranean (by D. Ninkovich and B. C. Heezen, 1965) supports this hypothesis regarding the season of the climax of the eruption. In addition, the distribution pattern of tephra accounts for the disaster brought about by the fall of ash in central and eastern Crete and, much further to the south-east, in lower Egypt.

Although this explanation is not pressed, it is nevertheless remarkable. The events take place in the same sequence as the natural phenomena which favour the events. The plagues precede the Exodus. The sea-wave which helped the Exodus of the Israelites was produced by the collapse of Santorin; and the collapse occurred after the eruption phenomena which brought about the plagues. The case certainly exists and seems amenable to test and proof. For those who believe that the plagues and the crossing of the waters were miracles of Divine Providence alone, the miracle, as Bennett remarks, lies in the timing of the occurrences, the synchronizing of events. Moses is divinely guided to take advantage of the mechanism of occurrences whose manifestation obeys natural laws which are themselves the work of God.

Bibliography

THROUGHOUT: Plato's *Timaeus* and *Critias*, the relevant passages of which are quoted in full in Appendix A.

INTRODUCTION
A list of the principal works on Atlantis may be found in the following:
J. Gattefossé and C. Roux, *Bibliographie de l'Atlantide et des questions connexes*, Lyon, 1926.
A. Bessmertny, *L'Atlantide: Exposé des hypothèses relatives à l'énigme de l'Atlantide*, trans. by Dr F. Gidon, Professor at the University of Caen, enlarged with a chapter by the translator on North Atlantic submersions in the Bronze Age and several other documentary pieces. Paris, 1949.
Colonel A. Braghine, *L'Atlantide*, Paris, 1952.

CHAPTER ONE
H. and G. Termier, *La trame géologique de l'histoire humaine*, Paris, 1961.
F. Gidon, 'Les submersions atlantiques (irlando-armoricaines) de l'âge du bronze et la question de l'Atlantide', *Mémoires de l'Académie des Sciences, Arts et Belles Lettres de Caen*, Caen, 1934.
H. Quiring, *Geschichte des Goldes (die goldenen Zeitalter in ihre kulturellen und wirtschaftilichen Bedeutung)*, Stuttgart, 1948.
Y. Reshetov, 'The Mythology of the Greeks in relation to the Atlantis Legend' (trans. E. Cordasco), *Atlantis*, Vol. 14, No. 5, London, 1961.
Sp. Marinatos, 'Le problème de l'Atlantide', *C. R. Soc. Hellén. d'Anthropologie*, Athens, 1948.
Geoffrey Bibby, *Four Thousand Years Ago*, London, 1961.

CHAPTER THREE
S. Marinatos, *loc. cit.*

CHAPTER FOUR
W. S. Broecker, 'Absolute Dating and the Astronomical Theory of Glaciation', *Science*, Vol. 151, 1966.
L. Donn and M. Ewing, 'A Theory of Ice Ages III', *Science*, Vol. 152, 1966.

M. Schwarzbach, 'Die Beziehungen zwischen Europa und America als geologisches Problem', *Sonderdruck aus Kölner Universitätsreden*, No. 23, Krefeld, 1959.

J. Rothé, 'La zone séismique médiane indo-atlantique', *Proc. Roy. Soc.*, Series A, Vol. 222, 1954.

B. C. Heezen and M. Ewing, 'The Mid-Oceanic Ridge and its extension through the Arctic Basin', *Geology of the Arctic*, Toronto, 1961.

D. Carr and L. Kulp, 'Age of a Mid-Atlantic Ridge Basalt Boulder', *Bull. Geol. Soc. Am.*, Vol 64, 1953.

C. Emiliani, 'Paleotemperature analysis of Core 230 and Pleistocene correlations', *Jour. Geology*, Vol. 66, 1958.

H. C. Hapgood, *Earth's Shifting Crust*, New York, 1958.

M. Rubin and H. E. Suess, 'US Geological Survey Radiocarbon Dates II (and III)', *Science*, Vol. 121, 1955; Vol. 123, 1956.

M. Ewing, X. Le Pichon and J. Ewing, 'Crustal Structure of the Mid-Oceanic Ridges: 4, Sediment Distribution in the South Atlantic Ocean and the Cenozoic History of the Mid-Atlantic Ridge', *Jour. Geoph. Res.*, Vol. 71, 1966.

D. B. Ericson, M. Ewing, W. Wollin and B. C. Heezen, 'Atlantic Deep-sea Sediment Cores', *Bull. Geol. Soc. Am.*, Vol. 72, 1961.

B. C. Heezen, 'Note of Progress in Geophysics, Dynamic Progress of Abyssal Sedimentation, Erosion, Transportation and Redeposition on the Deep-sea Floor', *Geophys. J. Roy. Astr. Soc.*, Vol. 2, 1959.

M. Ewing and W. L. Donn, 'A Theory of Ice Ages', *Science*, Vol. 123, 1956.

A. E. Scheidegger, *Principles of Geodynamics*, Berlin, 1958.

P. Termier, *A la Gloire de la Terre*, 2nd edn, Paris, 1924.

B. C. Heezen, M. Ewing and R. J. Menzies, 'The influence of Submarine Turbidity Currents on Abyssal Productivity', *Oikos*, Vol. 6, 1955.

R. Malaise, 'Oceanic Bottom Investigations and their bearings in Geology', *Geol. Fören*, Vol. 79, Stockholm, 1957.

B. C. Heezen and M. Tharp, 'The Atlantic Floor', *North Atlantic Biota and their History*, London, 1963.

J. R. Conolly and M. Ewing, 'Pleistocene Glacial-Marine Zones in North Atlantic Deep-sea Sediments', *Nature*, Vol. 208, 1965.

T. Saito, M. Ewing and L. H. Burckle, 'Tertiary sediments from the Mid-Atlantic Ridge', *Science*, Vol. 151, 1966.

J. A. Miller, 'Age Determinations on Samples of Basalt from the Tristan da Cunha group and other parts of the Mid-Atlantic Ridge', *Phil. Trans. Roy. Soc.*, London, A256, 1964.

A. Sieberg, 'Erdbebengeographie', *Gutenbergs Handbuch der Geophysik*, Vol. 4, Berlin, 1932.

B. F. Howell, Jr, *Introduction to Geophysics*, New York, 1959.

B. C. Heezen, M. Tharp and M. Ewing, 'The floors of the Oceans: 1, The North Atlantic', *Geol. Soc. Am.*, *Special Paper 65*, 1959.

F. P. Shepard, 'Submarine Canyons and Other Sea Valleys', *The Encyclopedia of Oceanography*, New York, 1966.

J. P. Rothé, 'La Structure de l'Atlantique', *Ann. di Geof.* Vol. 4, 1951.

M. N. Hill and C. J. Shallow, 'Seismic Experiments in the Atlantic', *Nature*, Vol. 165, 1950.

M. Båth, 'Crustal Structure in Iceland and surrounding Ocean', *ICSU Review*, Vol. 4, 1962.

Sir Edward Bullard, 'A Comparison of Oceans and Continents', *Proc. Roy. Soc.*, Series A, *Math.*, *Phys.*, *Sci.*, Vol. 122, 1954.

G. Dietrich and K. Kalle, *Allgemeine Meereskunde*, Berlin, 1947.

J. Bartels, 'Geophysik', *Das Fischer Lexikon*, Frankfurt-am-Main, 1960.

T. Einarsson, 'The Plateau Basalt Areas in Iceland', *On the Geology and Geophysics of Iceland*, ed. Sigurdur Thorarinsson, Reykjavik, 1960.

R. Dévigné, *Un Continent Disparu: l'Atlantide, sixième partie du Monde*, Paris, 1924.

H. E. Suess, 'Absolute Chronology of the last Glaciation', *Science*, Vol. 123, 1956.

W. R. Farrand, 'Postglacial Uplift in North America', *Am. Jour. Sci.*, Vol. 269, 1962.

D. Hafemann, 'Die Frage des Eustatischen Meeresspiegelansteigs in Historischer Zeit', *Verhandlunger des Deutschen Geographentages*, Vol. 32, Berlin, 1959.

Ph. Negris, 'L'Atlantide et la Regression quaternaire', *C.R. Acad. Sci.*, Vol. 174, Paris, 1922; 'Submersion et Regression Quaternaires en Grèce', *Bull. Soc. Geol. France*, Vol. 8, Paris, 1908.

F. Gidon, *loc. cit.*

H. and G. Termier, *loc. cit.*

Sir Gavin de Beer, *Reflections of a Darwinian*, Edinburgh, 1962.

W. Wolff, 'Ergebnisse einer Bereisung des Deutschen Nordseekuste zur Prüfung der Senkungsfrage', *Zeitschr.-Prakt. Geol.*, 1923.

H. Stille, *Grundfragen der Vergleichenden Tektonik*, Berlin, 1924.

J. Spanuth, *Das enträtselte Atlantis*, Stuttgart, 1953.

—, *Atlantis*, Tübingen, 1965.

G. Kehnscherper, 'Santorin—Traditionsgeschichtliche Untersuchungen uber Erinnerungen an die Santorinkatastrophe', *Apok*, 6, 8, 9, Leipzig, 1964.

Rhys Carpenter, *Discontinuity in Greek Civilization*, Cambridge, 1966.

P. Hédervári and I. Pados, 'Volcanophysical investigations concerning the energetics of the Minoan Eruption of Volcano Santorin', *Bulletin Volcanologique*, Vol. 25, Brussels, 1967.

C. Higgins, 'Causes of Relative Sea-level Changes', *American Scientist*, Vol. 53, 1965.

I. Velikovsky, *Worlds in Collision*, London, 1960.

A. Braghine, *L'Enigme de l'Atlantide*, Paris, 1952.

J. D. H. Wiseman, 'Geological and Mineralogical investigations: I. Basalts from the Carlsberg Ridge, Indian Ocean (with an appendix on the radium content of some sub-oceanic basalts from the floor of the Indian Ocean, by J. H. J. Poole), *John Murray Exp. Sci. Reports*, Vol. 3, London, 1937.

CHAPTER SIX

B. F. Howell, *Introduction to Geophysics*, New York, 1959.

W. C. Alden, 'Landslide and flood at Gros Ventre, Wyoming', *Trans. Am. Inst. Min. Met. Engrs.*, Vol. 76, 1928.

D. Torcher, 'The Hebgen Lake, Montana, earthquake of Aug. 17, 1959', *Bull. Seism. Soc. Am.*, Vol. 52, 1962.

Kuo Tseng-Chien, 'On the Shensi Earthquake of Jan. 23, 1956' (in Chinese with English abstract), *Acta Geophys. Sinica*, Vol. 6, 1957, in *Geophysical Abstracts*, 1958.

C. F. Richter, *Elementary Seismology*, San Francisco, 1958.

A. Sieberg, *Geologische, physikalische und angewandte Erdbebenkunde*, Jena, 1923.

Bortolli, *Essai sur l'explication historique donnée par Platon de sa république et de son Atlantide*, 1780.

Latreille, *Mémoires sur divers sujets de l'histoire naturelle des insectes, de géographie ancienne et de chronologie*, Paris, 1819.

L. Figuier, *La Terre et les Mers*, 4th edn, Paris, 1872.

K. T. Frost, 'The *Critias* and Minoan Crete', *Journal of Hellenic Studies*, Vol. 33, 1913.

D. A. Mackenzie, *Myths of Crete and Prehistoric Europe*, London, 1917.

E. S. Balch, 'Kreta or Minoan Crete', *Geog. Revue*, New York, 1917.

F. Butavandt, *La Véritable histoire de l'Atlantide*, Paris, 1925.

J. Koumaris, 'Atlantide et Atlantes (Etude basée sur les données plutot anthropologiques)', *C. R. Soc. Hellén. d'Anthropologie*, Athens, 1948.

Sp. Marinatos, 'Le probleme de l'Atlantide', *C. R. Soc. Hellén. d'Anthropologie*, Athens, 1948.

—, 'About the Rumour of Atlantis', *Cretika Chronika*, Vol. 4, Heraklion, 1950.

CHAPTER SEVEN

A. Philippson, *Beiträge zur Morphologie Griechenlands*, Stuttgart, 1930.

M. K. Mitsopoulos, 'Uber das Vorkommen von Elefante in der Aegais', *Prakt. Akad. Athen.*, Vol. 36, 1961.

A. G. Galanopoulos, 'On Mapping of Seismic Activity in Greece', *Ann. di Geof.*, Vol. 16, Rome, 1963.

J. Trikkalinos, 'Die Auswirkungen junger sehr starken diluvialen und rezenter orogener Bewegungen im Gebiete Griechenland', *Geotektonisches Symposium zu Ehren von Hans Stille*, Stuttgart, 1956.

Norman Douglas, *Looking Back*, London, 1933.

CHAPTER EIGHT

A. de Lapparent, *Traité de Géologie*, Paris, 1900.

H. Reck, *Santorin ; der Werdegang eines Inselvulkans und sein Ausbruch 1925–28*, Bd. III, Atlas (Kalderaprofil der Inselgruppe Santorin, von M. Neumann van Padang), Berlin, 1936.

C. Paparigopoulos, *History of the Greek Nation from the Ancient Times up to the Present*, Ed. A. Constantinides, Vol. I, Athens, 1885.

Sp. Marinatos, 'Amnisos, die Hafenstadt des Minos', *Forsch. und Fortschr.*, Vol. 10, 1934.

M. Pfannenstiel, 'Erläuterungen zu den Bathymetrischen Karten des östlichen Mittelmeeres', *Bulletin de l'Institut Océanographique*, No. 1192, Monaco, 1960.

R. W. Hutchinson, *Prehistoric Crete*, London, 1962.

C. G. Higgins, 'Possible Disappearance of Mycenean Coastal Settlements of the Messenian Peninsula', *Amer. Journ. Archaeol.*, 1966.

Sir Arthur Evans, *The Palace of Minos*, London, 1928.

G. Marinos and N. Melidonis, 'Über die Grösse des beim vorgeschichtlichen Ausbruch des Santorin-Vulkans ausgelösten Tsunamis', *Bull. Griech. Geol. Ges.*, Vol. 4, Athens, 1959–61.

J. P. Eaton, D. H. Richter and W. V. Ault, 'The Tsunami of May 23, 1960, on the Island of Hawaii', *Bull. Seism. Soc. Am.*, Vol. 51, 1961.

D. Miller, 'The Alaska Earthquake of July 10, 1958, Giant Wave in Lituya Bay', *Bull. Seism. Soc. Am.*, Vol. 50, 1960.

A. G. Galanopoulos, 'Tsunamis observed on the coasts of Greece from antiquity to the present time', *Ann. di Geof.*, Vol. 13, 1960.

V. Acylas, *Volcanoes and the Island Thera*, Athens, 1925.

H. Reck, 'Die Geologie der Ring-Inseln und der Kaldera von Santorin', *Der Werdegang eines Inselvulkanes und sein Ausbruch 1925 bis 1928*, Vol. 1, Berlin, 1936.

F. Press and D. Harkrider, 'Air-Sea Waves from the Explosion of Krakatoa', *Science*, Vol. 154, 1966.

Sir F. M. Bullard, *Volcanoes : in History, in Theory, in Eruption*, Edinburgh, 1962.

P. Hédervári, 'Volcanophysical Investigations Concerning the Energetics of the Minoan Eruption of Volcano Santorin', *Bulletin Volcanologique*, Vol. 25, 1967.

S. C. Blacktin, *Dust*, London, 1934.

M. Toperczer, *Geophysik*, Vienna, 1951.

Katô Yoshio et al., 'The Chile Tsunami of 1960 observed along the Sanriku coast of Japan', *Sci. Rep. Tôhoku Univ. 5: Geophysics*, Vol. 13, 1961.

Sp. Marinatos, 'The Volcanic Destruction of Minoan Crete', *Antiquity*, Vol. 13, 1939; *Crete and Mycenaean Greece*, Athens, 1959.

A. G. Galanopoulos, 'Zur Bestimmung des Alters der Santorin-Kaldera', *Ann. Géol. Pays Hellen.*, Vol. 9, 1958.

E. A. Olsen and W. S. Broecker, 'Lamont Natural Radiocarbon Measurement V', *Am. Jour. Sci. Rad. Suppl.*, Vol. 1, 1959.

J. G. Bennett, 'New Light on Atlantis and the Exodus', *Autumn Lectures*

1962, First Series—National Catastrophes that change History, Kingston-upon-Thames, 1962.

CHAPTER NINE

J. Schuster, 'Pflanzenführende Tuffe auf Santorin', *Santorin: der Werdegang eines Inselvulkans und sein Ausbruch 1925–1928*, H. Reck, Berlin, 1936.

C. G. Higgins, *loc. cit.*

J. F. Scott, *A History of Mathematics*, London, 1960.

Sir Edward Bullard, *loc. cit.*

S. C. Blacktin, *loc. cit.*

J. Bernstein, 'Giant Waves', *The World of Geology*, ed. L. D. and F. Leet, New York, 1961.

A. Rittmann, *Vulkane und ihre Tätigkeit*, Stuttgart, 1960.

M. Ventris and J. Chadwick, *Documents in Mycenaean Greek*, Cambridge, 1960.

J. Chadwick, 'The First Greek Script', *Ann. Sci. Fac. Phi. Univ.*, Vol. 12, Athens, 1962.

—, 'The Birth of the Greek Language', *Ann. Sci. Fac. Phi. Univ.*, Vol. 12, Athens, 1962.

P. Anagnostopoulos, 'The History of the Origin of the Olive Tree', *Prakt. Acad. Athens*, Vol. 26, 1951.

B. Eginitis, 'Le climat de la Crète et la constance du climat de la Grèce depuis l'époque de Minos', *Traités Acad. Athènes*, Vol. 18, 1954.

A. G. Galanopoulos, 'On the Origin of the Deluge of Deucalion and the Myth of Atlantis', *Greek Arch. Soc.*, Vol. 3 (in memory of G. Oekonomos), 1960.

—, 'On the Location and the Size of Atlantis', *Prakt. Akad. Athen.*, Vol. 35, 1960.

—, 'Die Deukalionische Flucht aus Geologischer Sicht', *Das Altertum*, Vol. 9, 1963.

—, 'Die ägyptischen Plagen und der Auszug Israels aus geologischer Sicht', *Das Altertum*, Vol. 10, 1964.

—, 'Tsunami', *Das Altertum*, Vol. 13, 1967.

—, 'Der Phaethon-Mythus im Licht der Wissenschaft', *Das Altertum*, Vol. 14, 1968.

N. N. Ambraseys, 'Data for the investigation of the Seismic Sea-waves in the Eastern Mediterranean', *Bull. Seism. Soc. Am.*, Vol. 52, 1962.

J. Garstang, *The Foundations of Bible History*, New York, 1931.

I. Velikovsky, *Worlds in Collision*, London, 1960.

P. Bratsiotis, *Introduction to the Old Testament*, Athens, 1937.

M. J. Schleiden, *Die Ländenge von Suez*, Leipzig, 1858.

H. Brugsch, *L'éxode et les monuments égyptiens*, Leipzig, 1875.

L. Cooper, *Aristotle, Galileo and the Tower of Pisa*, New York, 1935.

Annotated Bibliography on Tsunamis, *UGGI*, Monograph, 27 (1964), on the authority of Herodotus.

B. F. Howell, Jr, *Introduction to Geophysics*, London, 1959.

P. Saint-Amand, 'Los Terremotos de Mayo-Chile 1960'. China Lake, California: Michelson Laboratories, U.S. Naval Ordnance Test Station, *Technical Article 14*, NOTS TP 2701, August, 1961.

R. Takahasi and I. Aida, 'Studies of the Spectrum of Tsunamis', *Bull. Earthq. Res.Inst.*, Vol. 39, Tokyo, 1961.

A. Sieberg, *Erdbebenforschung und ihre Verwertung für Technik, Bergbau und Geologie*, Jena, 1933.

S. C. Blacktin, *loc. cit.*

J. G. Bennett, 'Geophysics and Human History', *Systematics*, Vol. 1, Kingston-upon-Thames, 1963.

F. V. Lane, *The Elements Rage*, Plymouth, 1966.

A. Rittmann, *loc. cit.*

D. Ninkovich and B. C. Heezen, 'Santorini Tephra', *Colston Papers*, Vol. XVII, London, 1965.

Notes on the Illustrations

Colour plates
Plate 1—Sigurdur Thorarinsson
Plates 2 and 21—Sigurgeir Jonasson
Plate 3—Athens Geological Museum (Photo A. G. Galanopoulos)
Plates 4, 5, 6, 7, 8, 10, 11, 12, 14 and 15 are from photographs taken especially for this book by D. A. Harissiadis (copyright © Thomas Nelson & Sons Ltd 1969)
Plates 9 (upper picture), 13, 16 and 17—Mrs Edward Bacon
Plate 9 (lower picture)—Roger M. Howlett
Plate 18—Leonard von Matt
Plates 19 and 20—Picturepoint
Plate 22—Professor Howell Williams
Plate 23—Oregon State Highway Department

Monochrome illustrations
The maps and diagrams on pages 34, 46, 55, 58, 63, 68, 69, 77, 78–9, 98, 101, 108–9, 128, 131 and 194 were drawn by Parfitt Mills and Associates. They are based in part on data supplied by the authors and in part on scientific publications cited in the Bibliography.
Page 13 Marble, no restorations, height 35·5 cm. Fitzwilliam Museum, Cambridge. Reproduced by courtesy of the Syndics of the Fitzwilliam Museum.
22 Photo William MacQuitty
23 Photo Sir Mortimer Wheeler
24 Iraq Museum, Baghdad. Photos Hirmer Verlag
25 Photo William MacQuitty
26 (top) Detail from the 'Harvesters Vase'. Black steatite, maximum diameter 11·5 cm, Late Minoan I. Archaeological Museum, Heraklion. Photo D. A. Harissiadis (copyright © George Rainbird Ltd 1968)
27 Photo Sir Mortimer Wheeler
28 (left) National Archaeological Museum, Athens. Photo D. A. Harissiadis (copyright © George Rainbird Ltd 1968)
28 (right) Ashmolean Museum, Oxford
29 Photos Alison Frantz
30 Photo Hirmer Verlag
31 Photo A. F. Kersting
32 Mansell Collection
37 Detail from a Protocorinthian olpe, the 'Chigi' vase, 7th century BC. Photo Hirmer Verlag
45 Detail of a portrait of Francis Bacon, from the studio of Paul Van Somer. National Portrait Gallery, London. Photo National Portrait Gallery
47 (top) Mansell Collection
48 Reproduced by courtesy of the Hutchinson Publishing Group Ltd
49 Culver Pictures Inc.
64 Photo National Institute of Oceanography, Wormley, Surrey
72 Photo Sigurgeir Jonasson
81 Photo Oriental Institute, University of Chicago
82 Fired clay, diameter 16 cm. Archaeological Museum, Heraklion. Photo Hirmer Verlag
84 Reproduced by courtesy of Faber and Faber Ltd
90 Mary Evans Picture Library
91 Photo Haroun Tazieff
92 Mansell Collection
94 After Perrot and Chipiez, *History of Art in Primitive Greece*, London, 1894
95 Terracotta, height 17·3 cm. Reproduced from Christian Zervos, *L'Art des Cyclades* (Paris, 1957), by courtesy of the publishers, Editions Cahiers d'Art
102 Photo Stephen Harrison

103, 105, 106 Photos D. A. Harissiadis (copyright © Thomas Nelson & Sons Ltd 1969)

111 Photo Karin Klein-Eriksson

117 (top) Mansell Collection

117 (bottom) Radio Times Hulton Picture Library

118 Reproduced from the *Illustrated London News* by courtesy of the London Electrotype Agency

119 Photo Nicos Kontos

120 Photo A. G. Galanopoulos

129 Reproduced from J. S. Morrison and R. T. Williams, *Greek Oared Ships 900–322 B.C.* (Cambridge University Press, London, 1968), by courtesy of the publishers

130 Reproduced from Dodwell, *Views and Descriptions of Cyclopean Remains in Greece and Italy* (1834)

132 Marble, no restorations, height 33 cm. Ny Carlsberg Glyptotek, Copenhagen. Photo Ny Carlsberg Glyptotek

136 Reproduced by courtesy of the executors of the late Sir Arthur Evans

139 Radio Times Hulton Picture Library

140 Photo Dr J. P. Olivier

141 Photo Edwin Smith

142 (top) Photo London Electrotype Agency, reproduced by courtesy of James Mellaart

142 (bottom) Reproduced by courtesy of the executors of the late Sir Arthur Evans

144 (top) Photo Hirmer Verlag

144 (bottom) Ashmolean Museum, Oxford

145 (top) Fresco from the Queen's Megaron, Palace of Knossos. Photo Hirmer Verlag

145 (bottom) Length 2·6 cm. Archaeological Museum, Heraklion. Photo Leonard von Matt

147 (top) Photo Hirmer Verlag

147 (bottom) Terracotta, length 20·5 cm, height 15 cm. Archaeological Museum, Heraklion. Photo Leonard von Matt

148 Black steatite (horns restored), height (without horns) 13 cm. Archaeological Museum, Heraklion. Photo Leonard von Matt

149 (top) Photo D. A. Harissiadis (copyright © George Rainbird Ltd 1969)

149 (bottom) Photo Arlette Mellaart

151 Photo D. A. Harissiadis (copyright © George Rainbird Ltd 1968)

152 Reproduced by courtesy of the executors of the late Sir Arthur Evans

154 Photo D. A. Harissiadis (copyright © Thomas Nelson & Sons Ltd 1969)

155 Ashmolean Museum, Oxford

156 (left) Terracotta, height 28 cm, Late Minoan I. Archaeological Museum, Heraklion. Photo Hirmer Verlag

156 (right) Ivory, height 3·2 cm, Early Minoan I. Archaeological Museum, Heraklion. Photo Hirmer Verlag

157 (left) Alabaster, height 19·8 cm. Reproduced from Zervos, op. cit., by courtesy of the publishers

157 (centre) Veined marble, height 30 cm. Archaeological Museum, Heraklion. Photo Leonard von Matt

157 (right) Black obsidian, height 28 cm. Archaeological Museum, Heraklion. Photo Leonard von Matt

158 Terracotta, white decoration, height 26·5 cm. Photo Hirmer Verlag

159 (top) Terracotta, white decoration, height 13·8 cm. Reproduced from Zervos, op. cit., by courtesy of the publishers

159 (bottom) Sword blade from Thera, National Museum, Copenhagen. Photo National Museum. Sword blade from Pylos, National Archaeological Museum, Athens. Photo D. A. Harissiadis (copyright © George Rainbird Ltd 1969)

160 Marble, height 17·3 cm (left-hand figure) and 15 cm, end of third millennium BC. Badisches Landesmuseum, Karlsruhe. Photo Badisches Landesmuseum

161, 162 Photos Miss E. K. Ralph, reproduced by courtesy of the University Museum, University of Pennsylvania

163 Photo James Mavor

164 (top left) Height 29 cm, Late Minoan I. Archaeological Museum, Heraklion. Photo Hirmer Verlag

164 (top right) Height 49·5 cm, Late Minoan II. Archaeological Museum, Heraklion. Photo Hirmer Verlag.

164 (bottom) Diameter 54 cm, Middle Minoan II. Archaeological Museum, Heraklion. Photo D. A. Harissiadis (copyright © George Rainbird Ltd 1968)

196 Photos A. G. Galanopoulos

Index

Page numbers in italic indicate an illustration of the subject.

Kok

●Oea

Cape Oea

Cape Perivola

THERASIA

NEA KAMENI

D

G

PALAEA KAMENI

ASPRONISI

Cape Akrotiri

0   1   2   3 *Miles*